D 2004
CW01084917
0031140053427
32/24 TRA

THE SHIP THAT CAME HOME

THE SHIP THAT CAME HOME

The Story of a Northern Dynasty

A.W. Purdue

III THIRD MILLENNIUM
PUBLISHING, LONDON

The Ship that Came Home

Copyright © 2004 A.W. Purdue

First published in 2004 by Third Millennium Publishing Limited,
an imprint of Third Millennium Information Limited

Farringdon House
105–107 Farringdon Road
London EC1R 3BU
United Kingdom
www.tmiltd.com

ISBN 1 903942 24 1

All rights reserved
No part of the contents of this book may be reproduced, stored in a retrieval system, or transmitted in any form or by any means, electronic, mechanical, photocopying, recording, or otherwise, without the written permission of Third Millennium Publishing.

Edited by Honeychurch Associates, Cambridge, UK
Designed by Anikst Design: James Warner
Produced by Third Millennium Publishing, an imprint of
Third Millennium Information Limited

Reprographics by DPI Colour Digital Ltd, UK
Printed and bound in Slovenia by Mladinska

Title page:
Anderson Place in the early nineteenth century
Artist unknown

Endpapers:
From Arthur Edward Blackett's game book

CONTENTS

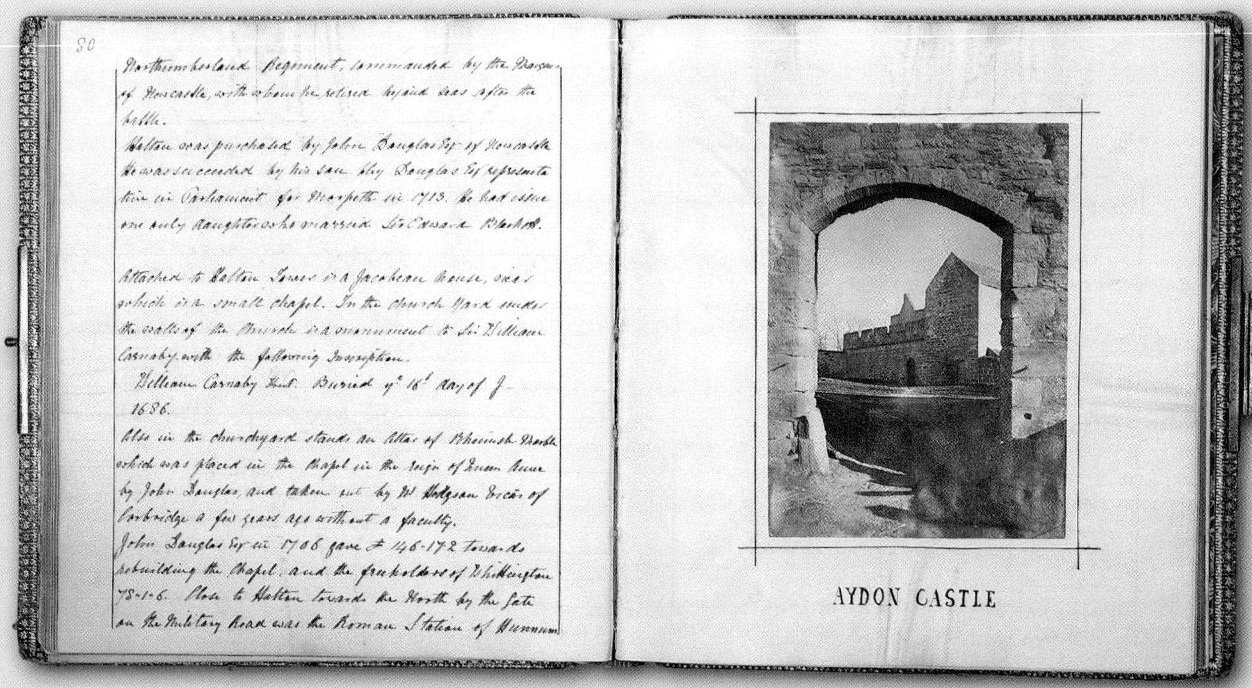
80

Northumberland Regiment, commanded by the Marquis of Newcastle, with whom he retired beyond seas after the battle.
Halton was purchased by John Douglas Esq of Newcastle He was succeeded by his son Oley Douglas Esq representative in Parliament for Morpeth in 1713. He had issue one only daughter who married Sir Edward Blackett.

Attached to Halton Tower is a Jacobean House, in which is a small chapel. In the Church Yard under the walls of the Church is a monument to Sir William Carnaby with the following Inscription.
William Carnaby Knt. Buried ye 16^t day of J-
1686.
Also in the churchyard stands an Altar of Rheinish Marble which was placed in the Chapel in the reign of Queen Anne by John Douglas, and taken out by Mr Hodgson Vicar of Corbridge a few years ago without a faculty.
John Douglas Esq in 1706 gave £ 146-17-2 towards rebuilding the Chapel, and the freeholders of Whittington 78-1-6. Close to Halton towards the North by the Gate on the Military Road was the Roman Station of Hunnum

AYDON CASTLE

FOREWORD

Three years ago Bill Purdue approached me to say that a manuscript, written by a Lady Blackett of Matfen in the 1880s, had been re-discovered in the South of England. Bill, who describes the genesis of the project in his Introduction, felt that it would form a wonderful basis for a book on the earlier Blacketts and the many houses with which they had been associated in Northumberland and beyond.

Bill's early enthusiasm was shared by Julian Platt, a London publisher with Northumbrian roots and a keen interest in northern subjects. As the idea developed I found no difficulty in sharing their commitment.

My first word of appreciation must be to Charles Sebag-Montefiore, who 'rescued' the manuscript, thereby making the book a possibility. He also kindly lent us the original for a protracted period. I am also most grateful for the enthusiastic support of the Compton family of Newby Hall.

I would also like to thank all those others who had a part in the book's creation – in particular Lindsey Shaw-Miller , our editor; Anikst Design, the designers; Duncan Davis, who took the marvellous contemporary photographs; and Bonnie Murray of Third Millennium who nursed the book through its production stages.

With Bill leading the way, we have together brought into being *The Ship that Came Home*. I will leave it to the reader to assess the value of our efforts.

Sir Hugh Blackett Bt.
Matfen Hall
October 2003

INTRODUCTION

The idea of this book was suggested by a manuscript discovered in a south country bookshop, far away from the stately home, Matfen Hall in Northumberland, where it was written. Charles Sebag-Montefiore, bibliophile, collector of rare books, treasurer to the London Library and other bookish charities, came across the leather-bound volume and bought it, as he puts it, 'to rescue it'. It was the work of Lady Blackett, wife of Sir Edward Blackett, 6th Bt. of Matfen in Northumberland.

Alethea Rianette Anne Scott, the daughter of Major-General Sir William Henry Scott and a granddaughter of Lord Stanley of Alderley, married Sir Edward Blackett, 6th Bt. of Matfen in 1880. She was his fourth wife. The marriage to her much older husband appears to have been a contented one, although her position was somewhat unusual as she had previously been jilted by her husband's eldest son, Edward William, and she clearly learned to love Matfen Hall and the surrounding Northumberland countryside. She came from a family that had Blackett antecedents[1] and her family home, Thorpe House, was close to the Blacketts' Surrey villa, Thorpe Lea. The Blackett family history and the many fine houses associated with it came to fascinate her.

It was, perhaps, the knowledge that life as the mistress of Matfen Hall would be brief that gave her the urge to write down details of the family's history, to gather together watercolours of the houses – many painted by her husband and some, presumably, by herself – as well as their interiors and surroundings, which belonged or had belonged to the Blacketts, and to take photographs. We can imagine that there may have been a certain poignancy attached to this work as, if she had married the son rather than the father, Matfen might have been her home for many years.

Like many Victorian ladies, she would have been an accomplished watercolourist, but her interest in the camera was less usual. The paintings and photographs in her book reveal Matfen Hall, commissioned and in part designed by her husband a half century earlier, as it was in the high age of the English country house. They evoke a period when, if the railways and improved roads had made rural areas like Tynedale more accessible, motor transport was still some decades away and country life still had a rhythm and culture of its own. Central to that way of life were big houses like Matfen. Set in the midst of large estates, they were the powerhouses for entire local economies. In one way or another, the local community depended wholly upon them; the tenant farmers and farmworkers, and the large number of indoor and outdoor servants that were needed to run the elaborate way of life of the gentry. The local churches were supported by the gifts and legacies of the gentry, and the livings of the clergy were often endowed and incumbents appointed by them. Entire landscapes were shaped to reflect the needs and tastes of the big houses and were sculpted for their views, their eye-catching details and the requirements of hunting and shooting.

Lady Blackett's interests reflected the enthusiasm of the late nineteenth century for family histories, and the determination of many families to get their genealogies exactly right. There was a growing interest in the histories of counties and cities, and in the notable families that had figured in them. Interest in the Blackett family's history was keen amongst family members, and Alethea's stepson, Lieutenant

William Blackett 1588 married Isabella Cro...

Christopher of Hoppyland. Edward. Sir William died 1680. 1st B. 1673.

2nd Sir Edward b. 1649 d. 1718. m. 2nd Mary Yorke.
Michael. m. Dorothy Barnes.
Sir William. Created Baronet 1684. died 1705. m. Julia Conyers.
Elizabeth Isabel William.

William ...1713
Edward. 3rd Baronet. died 1756 m. J. Jekyll.
John died 1750. m. Patience Wise.
Christopher. m. Jane Saville.
2nd Sir William m. Lady Barbara Villiers. no children. illegitimate dau. Elizabeth Orde
Julia m. Sir Walter Ca...

Edward. ... 1719. ... 1804 m. 1751. Anne Douglas.
William Henry John Erasmus
Patience m. to Mr Stanley
Edward Bridges 2
Julia m. 2nd Benjamin Scott
Sir Walter Calverley m. Elizabeth Orde Illegitimate d. of Sir William

5. Baronet.
...ne. ... Edward. b. 1752 d. 1796
...illiam Scott.
William died 1816. m. Mary Ann Keane.
William m. Anne Blackett.

- Christopher an officer in the army of King Charles I m. ...
... Thomas Fenwick of Matfen and dying in 1675 befo...
of Hoppyland for many years away at the Court of Swe...
... daughter of the duc de Boys, also John of Hopp...
m. Mary daughter & heir of John Errington of Er...
Beaufront, succeeded by the eldest son John B...
...

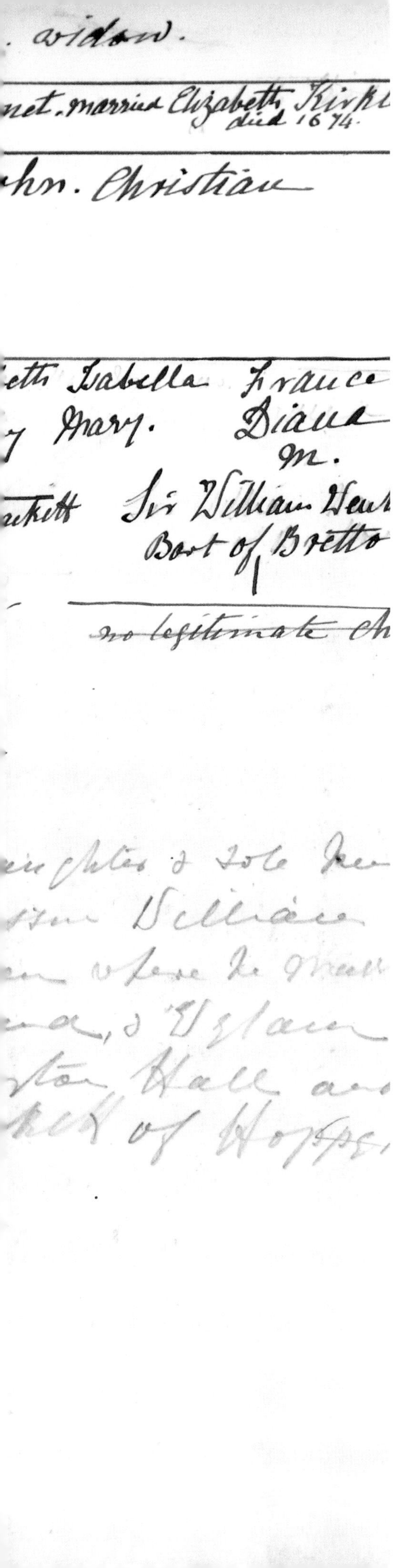

Family tree compiled by Alethea, Lady Blackett, in her book about Matfen Hall, *c.* 1880.

Above: Rickman's original drawing of his plan for Matfen Hall, 1832.

Right: The view from the drawing room at Matfen, painted in watercolour, from Lady Alethea's book.

Colonel Henry Wise Ridley Blackett, was compiling a similar volume of historical notes at about the same time; they may well have collaborated. Alethea was able to work from the family papers at Matfen, surrounded by the portraits of the people she was writing about, and was also able to benefit from the publications of the flourishing history societies, the Surtees Society and the Society of Antiquaries of Newcastle upon Tyne. Her delight in the houses associated with the Blackett family was also in tune with the concerns of her time. The watercolours and photographs, even more than her words, display a sophisticated eye for architectural detail and for the way houses relate to gardens and to the wider landscape, which resonates with her husband's architectural gift.

We cannot know her exact purpose in compiling her handwritten manuscript together with its illustrations. Very little of the contents are in her own words, and the work consists largely of a judicious collection of passages from a variety of secondary and some primary sources, together with genealogies. Similarly, the watercolours and drawings are by several hands. Her work may simply have been a hobby begun to while away the time, but she continued to collect information long after Sir Edward had died and she had remarried. It may have represented the notes and first drafts of a work she hoped to take further. Certainly there is an order to the manuscript, although there are sections that appear incomplete, while at the end there are copies of letters and other documents, which perhaps awaited incorporation into a fully developed book.

Alethea Blackett's marriage to Sir Edward lasted only five years as he died in 1885, and in 1888 she married Henry Frederick Gisborne Holt of Ropeley Grove, Hampshire,

THE SHIP THAT CAME HOME

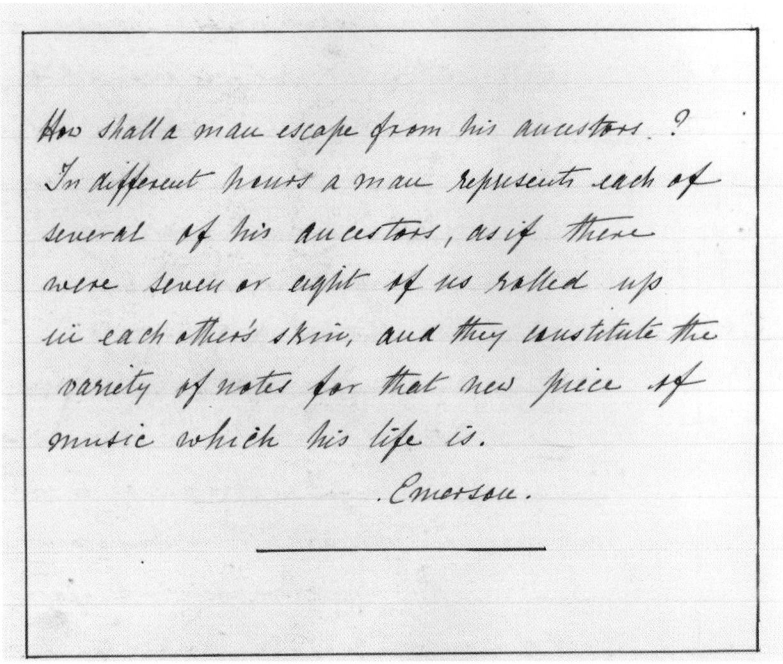
How shall a man escape from his ancestors?
In different hours a man represents each of
several of his ancestors, as if there
were seven or eight of us rolled up
in each other's skin, and they constitute the
variety of notes for that new piece of
music which his life is.
Emerson.

a man a little younger than she. The move to Hampshire may well explain why her manuscript became separated from other Blackett papers. That she continued with her research and carried on using her Blackett name and title suggests an abiding pride and interest in the Blackett family and perhaps a nostalgia for her short period as mistress of Matfen.

This present book aims not to reproduce her work, but rather to build upon her research and incorporate many of her illustrations and photographs into a short history of the Blackett family, which follows her lead in giving attention to the houses as well as the people. It seeks to see the family's history in the light of the work done by historians on the histories of Newcastle and Northumberland since Lady Blackett's time, and to be more concerned with social and economic history and the sources of the family's wealth than she was. It draws upon other photographs, paintings and documents in the possession of Sir Hugh Blackett, 12th Bt., including the architectural drawings for Matfen Hall. The position and perspective of her time and place is, nevertheless, respected, while I am much indebted to her research. Ironically, the person of whom we do not have a photograph or painting is Alethea. The book concludes with a section about the houses today, nearly 120 years after she left Matfen. I hope that she would have approved of it.

1. THE BLACKETTS OF NEWCASTLE AND WALLINGTON

To say that the Blackett family was among the most important and successful families of seventeenth-century Newcastle would be something of an understatement. Sir William Blackett Bt. (1621–1680) built up an immense fortune and was the unchallenged political leader of the town. He made enough money to found two dynasties, and he and his son William bestrode the town more like Renaissance princes than wealthy merchants. Few provincial merchants had a mansion within a town's walls, still less one like Grey Friars, the *rus in urbe* that became the Blacketts' seat, with its extensive grounds, formal gardens and a stream on its western border.

In the next century Blackett wealth, now increased by land with mineral riches below the surface, spread out westwards from Newcastle into vast estates and beautiful country houses, yet the family still retained its links with Newcastle, which returned Blacketts to Parliament from generation to generation.

The road to prosperity in early modern England was well mapped: a start in terms of parents of at least modest substance was usually essential; business acumen and perseverance were a necessity; advantageous marriage was more than useful; a sound constitution in the context of disease-ridden towns was crucial; while good luck, amidst the perils of a trading career, was the wild card. All these blessings were bestowed on Sir William Blackett, and perhaps something else: a touch of genius. The rise of the Blacketts was not untypical of the advance in fortune of many Newcastle families, save in the heights that were scaled.

Sir William Blackett's father, William Blackett (1588–1680), provided his three sons with the first steps on the road to economic and social advance, in the dynamic and expanding economy and relatively fluid society of the seventeenth-century north

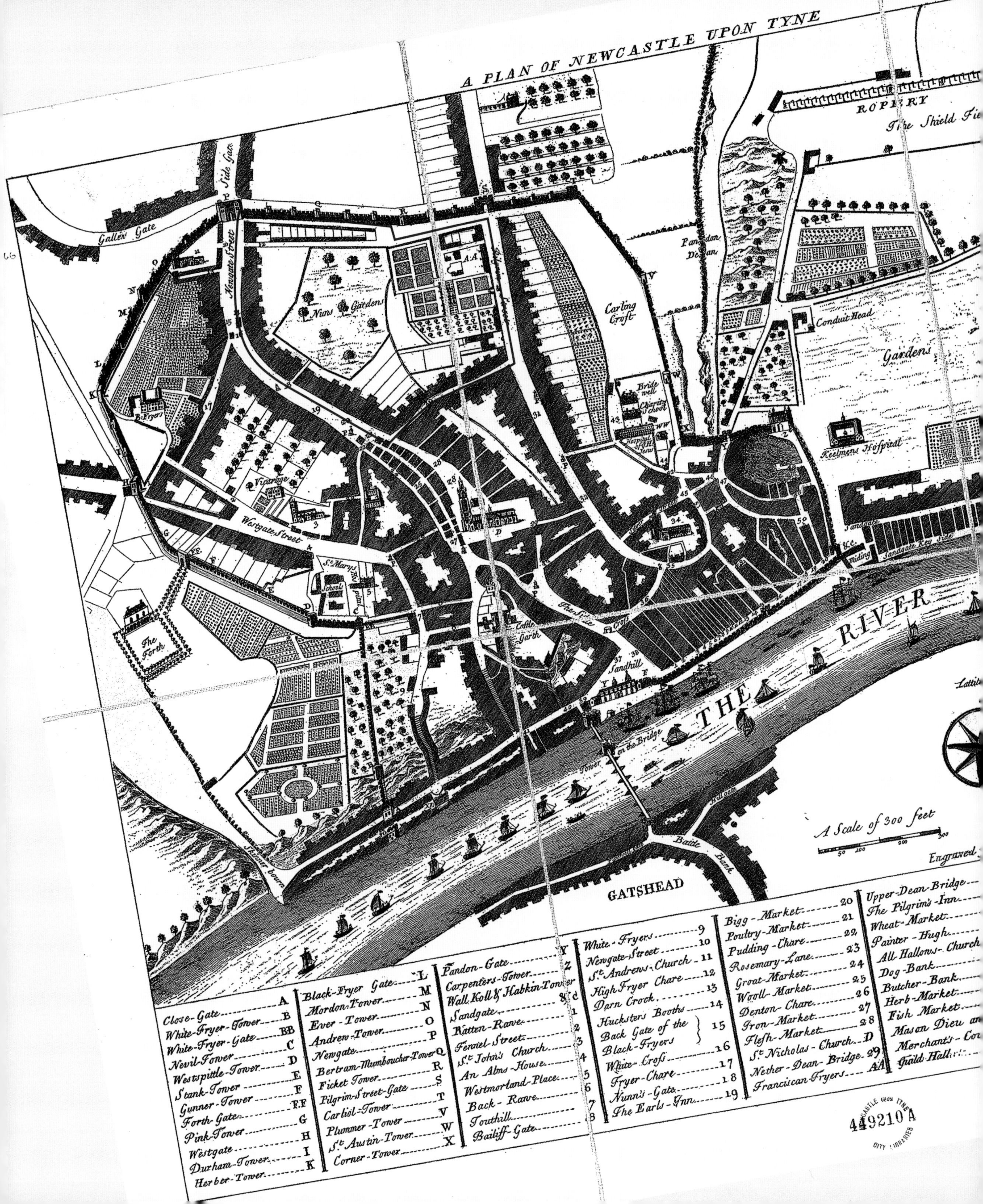

CASTLE UPON TYNE CITY LIBRARIES 449210 A

east. The elite was, indeed, open, if by elite we mean those numbered amongst the wealthier merchants and substantial gentry. It is true, nevertheless, that most of those who gained such status came from the immediately inferior echelons of yeomen, minor gentry or less substantial merchants. Such was William Blackett. The family seems to have come from the chapelry of Hamsterley, west of Bishop Auckland in County Durham, and to have been related to the Blacketts of Woodcroft. Hoppyland, close to Hamsterley, was purchased by William in 1619, but he or his forebears seem to have acquired interests and property scattered over a wide area, which included Tyneside and north Yorkshire. There were lead mines on some of his property, and the lead was taken to Jarrow by packhorses to be shipped. A man on the borderline of yeoman/gentry status, he had sufficient wealth and connections to enable him to

Henry Bourne's map of Newcastle from his book *The History of Newcastle upon Tyne* (1736), which was dedicated to the Mayor, Sir Walter Blackett, and other civic dignitories, shows the extent of the house and grounds of Blackett's mansion relative to the size of the town. *Newcastle upon Tyne City Libraries.*

Portrait of Sir William Blackett (1621–1680), 1st Bt.
Attributed to John Riley.

arrange the marriage of his eldest son, Christopher, to the heiress of Thomas Fenwick who owned land near Matfen, thus founding the line of the Blacketts of Wylam, and to arrange the admission of his younger sons as apprentices to the Newcastle Company of Merchant Adventurers.[2]

The Company of Merchant Adventurers formed the inner circle of Newcastle society. If apprenticeship by indenture was a lengthy and arduous process, an entrant, once he had his 'freedom' in the company, was in an advantageous position: all trade, 'foreign bought or sold', in or out of the town was reserved for its members. The exception was the coal trade, which, since the Elizabethan period, had grown rapidly, but most members of the Company of Hostmen, which controlled this most valuable trade, were also members of the Merchant Adventurers. Not surprisingly, prosperous families from a wide area were keen, despite the expense of indenture, to see younger sons apprenticed as Merchant Adventurers. The Bewicks, Carrs, Forsters, Herons, Shaftos, Ridleys and Bowes were among the many gentry families who sent sons to apprenticeships in Newcastle.

Edward Blackett commenced his apprenticeship in 1630, six years before his younger brother, William. He was apprenticed to John Butler. William's first master was William Sherwood, but he was transferred to Joane Carr, probably the widow of a merchant, in 1642 and admitted to the Merchant Adventurers in 1645. Edward was not admitted to the company until 1647, two years later than William. Edward's lengthy apprenticeship was due to his spending many years in Amsterdam, where he worked as a factor for various members of the company. This residence in the Low Countries was by no means unusual. Local knowledge

…igh wind.

started late owing to wet.

and connections were valuable assets, for successful trading depended upon good intelligence and also upon trust between trading partners. The great merchant houses of Europe invariably sent a son to reside in the towns with which they did business. Edward's position must have proved very useful to William, who, even before his apprenticeship was over, seems to have embarked on trade in his own right, and soon built up an extensive business with Holland and more distant markets such as Denmark, Hamburg and the Baltic, for all of which good Dutch connections were invaluable.

afternoon only.
Mr. Liddell came
at lunch time.
3 snipe on Thorn

That William was able to build up a successful business in Newcastle during the 1630s and 1640s is a tribute both to his ability and his good health. He started his apprenticeship in a year of plague, when about a third of Newcastle's inhabitants died. It was a difficult period for merchants. The town had to pay £60,000 to persuade the Scots to depart in 1640, and then in 1643 and 1644 had to endure first a blockade, and then siege and storming when they returned under General Leslie's command. Newcastle was in the eye of the Civil War, and the captive King Charles was housed in the mansion that William Blackett was later to own, but which then belonged to the town's MP, Sir Francis Anderson, a royalist whose collieries were sequestered by the Parliamentarians.

The Civil War, or Great Rebellion, occasioned political and religious passion in Newcastle, but it also allowed competing groups within the circles of its civic and economic life to settle scores and to seek power within the town. William Blackett was a royalist whose elder brother Christopher was an officer in King Charles's army, so he was in a vulnerable position. He survived by not entering into public

afternoon only.

Sir William Blackett 1st Bt.
A miniature at Wallington.
The Trevelyan Collection
(The National Trust)
Brenda Norrish

life, while he had, like most people, relatives on the opposing side, which usually afforded some protection to those who kept their heads down.

Through these turbulent years, he steadily built up his seaborne trade. War with the Dutch in 1652 must have added an extra peril to the already dangerous business of trade in the North Sea and the Baltic. The most carefully planned enterprises could founder on bad debts, ruined cargoes or sunken ships. The Baltic and the passage out of it through the Sound were particularly risky for ships in the winter months. Luck and the ability to take advantage of it were inseparable from success in business. What made William Blackett's first fortune was, it is said, a ship that came home. The following embroidered and romanticized account describes this episode:

Sir William, soon after he commenced business, risked his little all, in a speculation in flax, and having freighted a large vessel with that article, received the unpleasant intelligence that the flax fleet had been dispersed in a storm, and most of the vessels either lost or afterwards captured by the enemy. He took his accustomed walk next morning, ruminating on his supposed loss, and unconscious how far he was going, when on a sudden, he was aroused, by the noise of a ship in the river: he jumped upon an adjoining hedge, hailed the vessel, and found it to be his own, which had miraculously weathered the storm, and with difficulty had gained the port. He instantly returned, and hiring a horse, rode in a very short time to London, and hastening to the Exchange, found the merchants in great alarm about the loss of the flax fleet, and speaking of the consequently high price of flax. On informing them that he dealt in that article, and had a large quantity to dispose of, speculators soon flocked around

Alethea Blackett's handwritten copy of John Straker's version of the foundation of the Blackett fortune in his *Pedigree of the Family of Blackett.*

him, and he sold his whole cargo at a most extravagant price, and the produce of that adventure laid the foundation for one of the largest fortunes acquired in Newcastle.[3]

He must have already built up a business and been seen as a coming man when he finished his nine years' apprenticeship in 1645, for he immediately married Elizabeth Kirkley. Her father had died when she was a child but her mother, another Elizabeth, had carried on his business and had prospered. This was a shrewd alliance, for his wife was connected to most of the ruling families of the town, both the temporarily marginalized royalist families of the old elite, and the puritan families that prospered with the coming of the Commonwealth. Her elder sister had married a Bonner, and Thomas Bonner was an important Presbyterian member of the puritan faction which controlled Newcastle during the interregnum. William Blackett and Elizabeth were to have eleven children, seven of whom survived into adulthood.

Whatever their differences, there was one thing puritans and royalists in Newcastle agreed on: the necessity of protecting the privileges of the town and its companies. These came under threat from two quarters. The London trading companies had long resented the independence of the Newcastle Company of Merchant Adventurers and its successful trade with foreign ports, while other ports on the Tyne resented Newcastle's monopoly of trade and its control of the river, as, indeed, did coastal harbours and ports on nearby rivers. That Blackett's ability was respected is shown by his membership of the four-man delegation which the Merchant Adventurers sent to London in 1656, to petition Parliament against threats to its

[le]ast doubt of its authenticity:

[Br]illiance, soon after he commenced business, risked [his] little all, in a speculation in flax, and hav[ing] freighted a large vessel with that article, received the unpleasant intelligence that the flax fleet had been dispersed in a storm, and most of the vessels either lost or afterwards captured by the enemy:— He took his accustomed walk next morning, ruminating on his supposed loss, and unconscious how far he was going, when on a sudden, he was aroused, by the noise of a ship in the river; he jumped upon an adjoining ledge, hailed the vessel, and found it to be his own, which had miraculously weathered the storm, and with difficulty had gained the port. He instantly returned, and hiring a horse, rode in a very short time to London, and hastening to the Exchange, found the merchants in great alarm about the loss of the flax fleet, and speaking of the consequent high price of flax. On informing them that he dealt in that article, and had a large quantity to dispose of, speculators soon flocked round him, and independence. Along with his brother Edward, he was from 1652 a member of the Hostmen's Company, and although he had interests in coal mines himself, he was able to make good profits by acting as the agent for other coal-owners who were not Hostmen. He was, therefore, both as a Merchant Adventurer and a Hostman, an implacable opponent of the coal owners who were not members of the Newcastle companies and who found a champion in Ralph Gardner of North Shields. Gardner's *England's Grievance Discovered* (1655) powerfully articulated the case for the other ports on the Tyne that resented Newcastle's monopolies. Fortunately for Newcastle and its companies, the Restoration was to put an end to such threats for the time being, and the monopolies continued.

As the Commonwealth weakened and pressure for the restoration of the monarchy grew, so the dominant puritan faction in Newcastle grew nervous, and royalists became bolder. William Blackett was elected Sheriff in 1659, but declined the honour. By 1660 he was more confident and accepted. The Mayor, John Emmerson, was a puritan, to whose lot it fell to welcome General Monck and his army, harbingers of the Restoration. One can imagine that Blackett took some pleasure in the Mayor's discomfiture, for a decade earlier Emmerson had called him 'an interloupeing giddy headed fellow, sayeing three or four times he lyed in his throate'[4]. A few months later, as Welford puts it, 'tar barrels were burning and Mr Sheriff Blackett was spending £22 for a tun of wine to run through a pant in honour of the coronation of his sacred Majesty King Charles II'.[5]

Now William Blackett came into his own. He became an Alderman, a captain in the militia and a Commissioner of Assessment. He was Governor of the Hostmen's

Company in 1662–63 and 1667–68, Mayor in 1666 and, after the death of that sturdy royalist Sir John Marley, he was elected as one of Newcastle's two MPs in 1673. That this pleased King Charles was evident, for Blackett was made a baronet within the week.

As civic and national honours were conferred upon him, his economic fortunes increased. The old alchemists had tried to turn lead into gold, but the high price of lead in the last half of the seventeenth century enabled several men to do this successfully, and Blackett was one of them. He bought the estate of Slaley from John Forster and Henry Ridley in 1668, and the Dukesfield and Colepitts estates from the Widdringtons. His 'West Water' estate, between Haydon Bridge and Haltwhistle, was also rich in lead. He then turned his attention to what were to be the lead-rich seams of the Allen Valley and Upper Weardale. Allendale belonged to Sir Francis Radcliffe, and Weardale to the Bishop of Durham, and Blackett took leases from them. He not only smelted his own ore at his great smelt-mills at Dukesfield and Planking, but ore from the mines of others. His monthly pay bill was about £630, something of a problem as there was a shortage of coinage throughout the late seventeenth century; but Blackett simply minted his own copper coins with which to pay his workforce.

Like most successful merchants in this period, his economic interests were wide. Lead might well be the most profitable of his enterprises, but he possessed coal mines on the manor of Winlaton, which he purchased, and others at Kenton to the north of Newcastle, while continuing as a merchant to trade in diverse goods. It may have been sentiment which made him buy the manor of Woodcroft, where generations of Blacketts had lived, but he also bought Sockburn, near Darlington, which had for centuries been the seat of the Conyers family. Like so many families, they had been ruined by a loyalty to their king during the Civil War which was ill-rewarded at the Restoration.

Grey Friars, or Newe House, also called Anderson Place, in 1812.

Even before he became its MP, he was the foremost representative of Newcastle's interests. In 1662 he became a member of the Eastland Company, which specialized in the Baltic trade, in London, and attended its general meeting on behalf of the Newcastle members. He acted on behalf of the Merchant Adventurers when its dispute with the London Merchant Adventurers was heard by the Royal Council in 1674, and when a compromise between the two companies was discussed in the same year.

While he was Mayor in 1666–67, he demonstrated his good sense and feeling for popular opinion when he quelled a riot in Newcastle occasioned by the hearth tax. This tax was introduced in 1662 and was paid twice a year at the rate of two shillings per hearth or fireplace, though exemption on grounds of poverty was possible. Trade was slack and times were hard for the keelmen of Sandgate, and when the collectors of the hearth tax went into Sandgate they were driven out 'with curses threats and stones'. Blackett made a conciliatory speech, arguing that the tax was small and only those who could afford to would be made to pay. When the residents replied that they had no bread but were living off oatmeal and boiled water, Blackett promised that only those willing to pay should be taxed. The tumult subsided and the government was informed that all had been quieted by the prudence of the Mayor and the Commissioners.

He was elected MP three times, in 1673, 1678 and 1679, and, if not active in parliamentary debates, he was a member of many committees. He seems to have rather resented

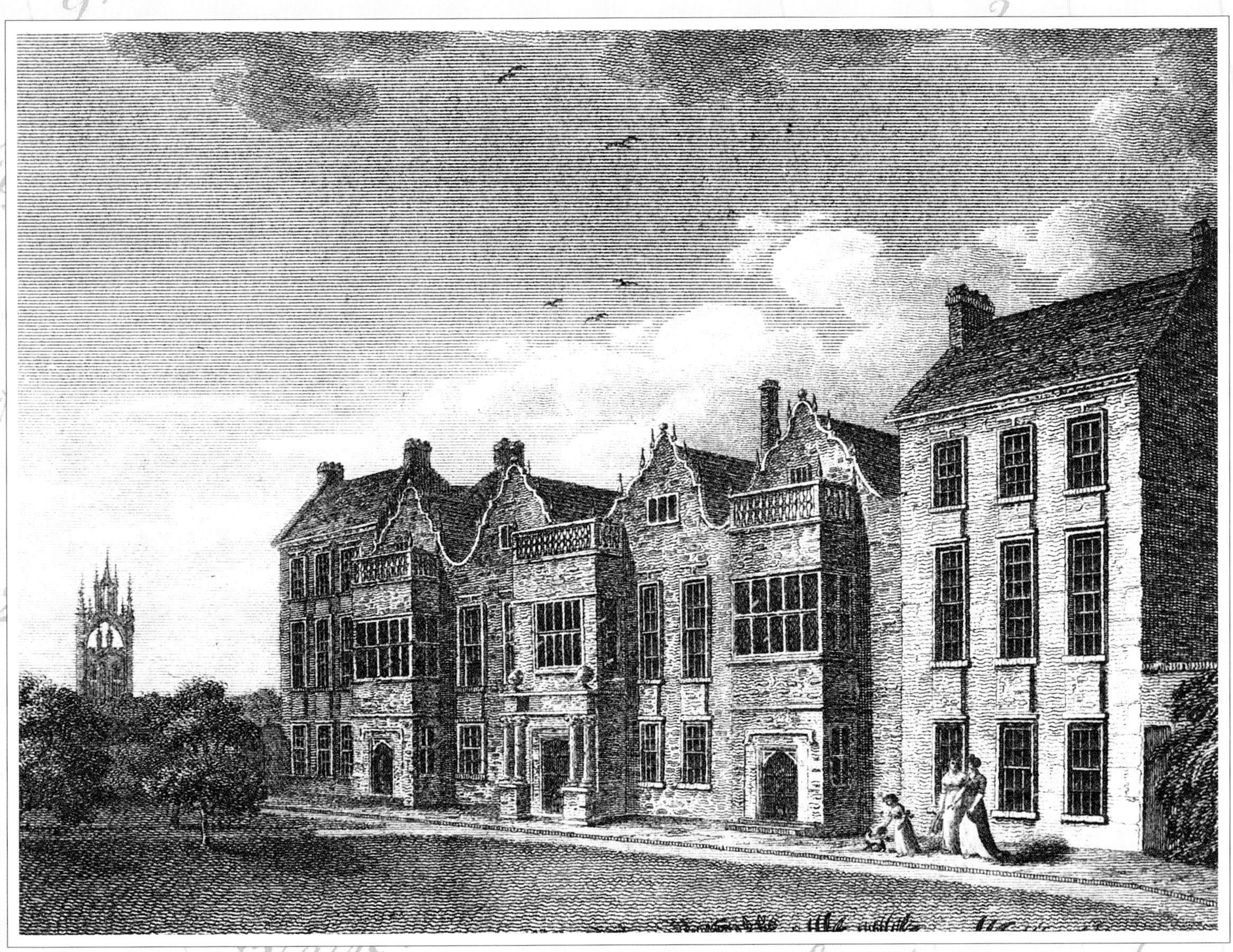

THE SHIP THAT CAME HOME

The following is a quote from *'From the History of Newcastle'* featured in Lady Alethea's book: 'On the right hand, passing down Pilgrim Street, stood a noble mansion which was built in 1580 by Robert Anderson, merchant, out of the offices and nearly upon the site of the Franciscan priory. He bought the property of Lady Gaverne. The house was selected for the Head Quarters of General Lord Leven during the captivity of King Charles I in Newcastle. Sir Francis Anderson Knt in 1675 sold the property to the first Sir William Blackett, Baronet of Wallington who added two wings to it. It came into the possession of Sir Walter Blackett Bt. by his marriage with Sir William's Grand daughter. In 1782 it was sold to Mr. George Anderson, an opulent architect, whose son Major Anderson called it Anderson Place. He sold the house to the corporation of Newcastle.'

The grand entrance to Anderson Place in 1825.
Newcastle upon Tyne City Libraries.

a good many. windy.

Fearfully hot saw no partridges. Pointer would not work.

Very hot again 2 mallards 1 teal

Got 4 pike & lost a good one.

Very hot & sultry.

time spent away from Newcastle and his business affairs. However, when his own and his town's interests were threatened, he responded rapidly; thus when there was a proposal for a ballast shore at South Shields, he got to his feet and made a speech opposing it. The bill was defeated.

By the time of the death of his wife, Elizabeth, in 1674, his sons and daughters were adults. In that year the eldest son, Edward, married the heiress to Thomas Norton of Langthorne, Yorkshire. The eldest daughter, Elizabeth, was already married to William's close friend, William Davidson, who was Mayor of Newcastle. The second and third sons, Michael and William, were both active in the family business. The following year Sir William remarried. His bride was Margaret, the daughter of Henry Cocke and the widow of Captain John Rogers of Denton. The Cockes were a very rich and well-connected Newcastle family, so wealthy that the daughters of the leading member of the family, Alderman Cocke, gave rise to the Newcastle saying 'as rich as Cocke's canny hinnies'.

The second marriages of a wealthy parent are not always welcomed by the children of the first marriage. Michael, hitherto his father's right arm in business, seems to have felt that he was being pushed out as the new Lady Blackett exercised her influence. This lady seems also to have encouraged Sir William to adopt a grander lifestyle. He had lived in a house to the west of the Mansion House, in the Close, the street in which many of the Newcastle elite lived. It was a fine old house with gardens sloping down to the river. About the time he married Margaret, he purchased the town's greatest mansion, Grey Friars, from his fellow MP, Sir Francis Anderson, and took to travelling in a grand coach.

wet morning went out after lunch.

Lovely shooting day.
1 weasel.

Bird very wild but saw
a good many. windy.

Fearfully hot saw no
partridges. Pointer would not work.

Armstrong & Walker
The Mansion of the late Sir Walter Blackett Bart.

Anderson Place, engraved by G. Sonander *c.* 1780.

Grey Friars, the Newe House or Anderson Place, as it was known at different times, was unique. In no other provincial town was there anything quite like the mansion, set in extensive grounds that took up so much of the walled town of Newcastle. London, of course, had its great mansions with spacious grounds, but these were outside the walls of the city. Robert Anderson had bought the land on which had once stood the Franciscan Friary in Pilgrim Street and the adjacent St Bartholomew's Nunnery, forty years after the dissolution of the two religious houses. He filled up the dene of the Lort Burn which intersected the grounds, and built what Grey in his *Choriographia*, the first history of Newcastle, called a 'princely mansion'. The house and grounds covered more than twelve acres, which extended from Pilgrim Street to Newgate Street, came close to the town walls to the north and had Upper Dean Bridge on its southern boundary.

The house provided a comfortable place of captivity for Charles I, who was lodged there for ten months following his surrender to the Scots in 1646. The king was at first allowed limited freedom and was able to play golf on Shield Field outside the town walls. An attempt to escape resulted, however, in his being largely confined to the house. According to Brand, a room in the house was known as the King's Bedchamber and contained the bed in which King Charles was supposed to have slept. The bed was said to have been sold by 'an incurious domestic' while the last owner was away on the Grand Tour.[6]

Sir William enjoyed this grandeur for only a few years as he died in 1680. His will suggests that relations with his wife were strained, for she was but modestly provided for. His third son, William, had clearly become his favourite; he was the sole executor and inherited much more than his elder brother Edward, the new baronet. Edward had already received a considerable settlement at the time of his marriage in the form of the 'West Water' estate, between Haltwhistle and Haydon Bridge, to which was now added the manor of Melkridge and Woodhall, near Haltwhistle, and the lead mines of Fallowfield and Acomb. Michael had also received a substantial marriage settlement and he was left in the will, a share in property at Winlaton which accrued to his brothers when he died childless in 1683. As Sir William's descendant Sir Charles Trevelyan put it, he made 'two elder sons' by leaving to William his Newcastle property, the bulk of his lead-rich estates west of Newcastle and, after the bequests to other brothers and sisters, the residue of his estate.

There were now to be three major Blackett families: the Blacketts of Wylam, springing from Sir William's elder brother, Christopher; the line from Sir Edward Blackett, 2nd Bt., who had acquired Newby Hall, near Ripon; and the line from William Blackett, now ensconced in Grey Friars and soon to own Wallington Hall.

Portrait of Sir William Blackett, 1st Bt. of Wallington (1647–1705). *Wallington, The Trevelyan Collection (The National Trust) Derrick E. Witty.*

Sr: WILLIAM BLACKETT. Bart:
created: Bart: Jan: 23. 168
Obt: Dec: 1705.

JULIA. Lady CONYERS.
Dr. of Rd. Viscount. LUMLEY.

SIR WILLIAM BLACKETT OF WALLINGTON 1647-1705

As we have seen, William, the third son of the first Sir William Blackett, was well provided for in his father's will. Although the eldest son, Sir Edward, received a handsome inheritance, William received rather more, perhaps in recognition that he had inherited the father's business acumen. To William went the Grey Friars mansion and other houses in Newcastle; estates at Killhope and Wellhope in Weardale and at Allendale, all rich in lead; leases on lead mines around Alston, the old family property, Woodcroft Hall, near Stanhope, and on collieries at Newburn, Kenton and elsewhere.

His inheritance alone made him a leading citizen of Newcastle and a figure of national importance because Newcastle, which warmed the hearths of London and retained considerable strategic significance, was important to the government. Newcastle made William an alderman and, without his holding the usual intermediate office of sheriff, elected him mayor in 1683 and, almost as important, Governor of the Hostmen in 1684. Charles II, who had only a few weeks to live, responded by creating him a baronet. Four days later he married Julia Conyers, granddaughter of Lord Lumley, and was elected MP for Newcastle in the following year.

If his father had been a strong Tory, the second Sir William was at first a moderate Tory and then a moderate Whig. It was circumstances, and the self-defeating policies of James II, that made Blackett a Whig. James's determination to reconstruct local government to his liking, and to fill the senior positions in the towns with Catholics or dissenters who might have their first loyalty to him, in place of the normal Anglican establishment, caused strife and unease throughout the land.

Portrait of Julia Conyers (m.1685, d.1705), wife of Sir William Blackett and granddaughter of Lord Lumley.
Wallington, The Trevelyan Collection (The National Trust) Derrick E. Witty.

Decorative plasterwork recovered from Anderson Place.

Even before the death of Charles II, the process of bringing the counties and towns to heel had begun. Newcastle's charter was recalled and the new charter of 1684 extended the royal veto on civic appointments. Sir William Blackett, who, like most Newcastle burgesses, was more concerned about the freedom and prosperity of his town than about national politics, found himself reluctantly taking on the role of champion of the town against overbearing royal authority. James forced the merchant adventurers and Hostmen to admit the outsider, Irishman and Catholic Sir William Creagh[7] to membership in 1686, and in the following year had the Mayor, Sheriff and a swathe of aldermen and councillors removed from office, replacing them with Catholics and nonconformists. A new charter restricted the parliamentary electorate to those whom the king thought might be amenable to his policy of abolishing the penal laws against religious dissent. It was clear, however, that even this group was about to re-elect Sir William Blackett rather than the king's preferred candidate, Nicholas Cole, at the election due to be held in November 1688. It never took place because of the landing in England of William of Orange and the subsequent flight of King James. The Glorious Revolution was popular in Newcastle, and the statue of James II, only erected a few years earlier, was tumbled into the Tyne. Blackett's reputation was enhanced. His record in elections was remarkable, for he won every one he contested and sat in five of the nine parliaments between 1685 and his death in 1705.[8]

During his father's lifetime William had lived in Kenton Hall, a short distance across the Town Moor from Newcastle, but he lost little time in moving. As we have seen, Grey Friars, or the Newe House (later Anderson Place), purchased by his father, was

The staircase from Anderson Place.

the grandest house in Newcastle; the second Sir William determined to make it even grander. Around 1690 he added two large brick-built wings with sash windows to the property. The result was a house in classical style, redolent of London houses of the period and rivalled in Newcastle only by the Mansion House of 1691. It was up-to-date in both materials and style, for brick was the acme of fashion in the Newcastle of the time. This was a suitable setting for the town's foremost citizen:

> *Here has Sir William, his lady and his guests, oftentimes paraded on the chequered pavement in the front of the house, or wandered to the brink of the stream which skirted the western boundaries of his gardens, or on his electioneering quests, entertained a thousand or so of the brethren of the Incorporated Companies, his constituents, or entered his golden coach drawn by horses six.*[9]

John Brand, the eighteenth-century historian of Newcastle, emphasized the way in which the extensive grounds concealed the mansion, and described their splendour:

> *That part of it* [the ground] *which faces the street is thrown into walks and grass-plots, beautified with images and beset with trees, which afford a very pleasing shade; the other part of the ground, on the west side of it, is all a garden, exceedingly neat and curiously adorned with statues and several other curiosities...*[10]

In addition to Anderson Place, Sir William, first baronet of his line, also owned Kenton Hall and its surrounding estate, but he was not content to be merely the

richest merchant and most influential man in Newcastle. Like many a Newcastle merchant before and after his time, he aspired to broad acres and the status of country gentleman. He purchased the Wallington estate from Sir John Fenwick in 1688 and shortly afterwards served as High Sheriff for Northumberland. This office was one which many county gentry dreaded, as it entailed great expense to the holder, but it was a mark of status. His purchase was not merely a country house and a few acres of parkland, for it included much of the land for miles around Hexham, the manor of Hexham having been bought by Sir John Fenwick's grandfather. As Welford has put it:

To the ample inheritance derived from his [Sir William Blackett's] *father, he added by the transaction the demesne, the mills, tolls and tithes of Hexham; the townships or farms of Dotland Park, Yarridge, Broomhaugh, Stagshaw Close, Anick Grange, Fenwick, Wallington, Harterton Hill, Cambo, Gunnerton, Coldwell, Rothley, Catcherside, Sweethope, Newbiggin, Greenleighton, Harwood House, Farney Law, Longwitton etc; the tithes of Slaley, Gunnerton and Coastley; the cornmills of Wallington, Gunnerton, Rothley and Sweethope; the rectory of Allendale; and the collieries of Hexham, Gunnerton and Kirkheaton.* [11]

There can rarely have been such a bargain. The Fenwicks were an ancient line who had never stinted in either their lavish hospitality or their loyalty to the Stuart kings. As a result Sir John was much in debt and suspected of being a rebel by the government. He was first of all forced to sell his lead mines to Sir William and then the whole Wallington estate. For the latter he received the settlement of his debts, which amounted to £4000, and an annuity for himself and his lady of £2000.

Fenwick was not only a supporter of the exiled King James but also a rash and incautious one. His brother-in-law, Viscount Preston, Lord President of the Privy Council in the last years of James's reign, had been involved in a number of plots aimed at restoring the king. When Preston was attainted and gaoled in 1689, Fenwick was also briefly imprisoned. Fenwick's house in London was well known as the haunt of the most flagrant Jacobites. He was too open to be a good conspirator, even ostentatiously refusing to doff his hat to the Queen Mary one day as she rode in Hyde Park. He was, inevitably, on the list of those usual suspects who were rounded up after the invasion plot of 1692 was discovered, but managed to remain in hiding until the crisis passed. In 1696 he was arrested for being part of a conspiracy to assassinate King William and mount a rising in the north east. He was probably guilty, but the evidence against him was weak as the only witness was a double agent and government informer. He was, nevertheless, attainted and executed. He had not enjoyed his annuity for long, and among those who voted for the Bill of Attainder in the House of Commons was the man who paid the annuity, the MP for Newcastle Sir William Blackett. Fenwick had his revenge, however, albeit on the king, not Blackett. King William met his death when his horse stumbled upon a molehill, causing Jacobites thereafter to toast the 'little gentleman in black velvet'. The horse King William was riding was a fine white racehorse, White Sorel. It had been confiscated from Sir John Fenwick.

Sir William was proud and fond of Wallington. Like so many rich men he was a great improver of his houses and, just as he had added new wings to Anderson Place, he set about rebuilding Wallington almost as soon as he had acquired it. The Fenwicks had, like many Northumberland families, such as the Herons at Chipchase and the

Portrait of Sir William Blackett, 2nd Bt. of Wallington (1689–1728). *Wallington, The Trevelyan Collection (The National Trust) Derrick E. Witty.*

Middletons at Belsay, built a manor house on to the existing tower, thus cautiously keeping one foot in the older world, where defence was essential, and the other in the emergent world, where comfort was important. Sir William erected what Sir Charles Trevelyan described as 'a residence on the model of a great French château, standing almost exactly square to the points of the compass, with four equal faces, each of them 120 feet in length'.[12] He spent much of every summer there, but also stayed occasionally at Hexham Priory (known also and variously as Hexham Abbey, Abbey House or Prior's House), another house he had gained with his purchase of Fenwick's estate.

Blackett died in London in December 1705 and his body was brought back to Newcastle in stately procession. Twelve persons on horseback attended the corpse as the funeral procession passed through the towns between London and Newcastle.[13] The funeral in Newcastle was conducted with great pomp and considerable expense, as befitted one who had been the town's leading citizen. Sir Henry Liddell, Lionel Vane, Mark Shafto, Ralph Carr and Nicholas Ridley were the pall bearers, who carried Sir William Blackett's coffin into St Nicholas's Church, where he was buried.

SIR WILLIAM BLACKETT OF WALLINGTON 1689-1728

Sir William came into his inheritance at the age of sixteen. As well as wealth and property, he automatically inherited status, as can be seen from the fact that as soon as he was twenty-one he was elected as one of Newcastle's two MPs. Perhaps the air of Wallington still carried Fenwick attitudes and traditions, for the young

...ning went...
shooting day.
1 weasel..

...d very wild but saw
...ood many. windy.
...rfully hot saw no
...ridges. Pointer would not work.
...y hot again 2 mallards 1 teal
...d one.
...t a pike & lost

Very hot & sultry

44

baronet was a very different man from his father. He was rather better at spending
money than making it, and he turned his back on his father's Whig convictions,
becoming a strong Tory with Jacobite sympathies. His father had entertained well,
but, with the son's reign at Wallington, it was a time for roisterous parties, which
recalled the days of the Fenwicks. Six servants remained after dinner for the express
purpose of carrying drunken guests to their beds.

His entry into Newcastle's political life came with a general election, which was held at a
time of strong party feeling. Blackett and Sir William Wrightson challenged the sitting
Whig members, William Carr and Henry Liddell. A Tory song celebrated the ensuing
Tory victory. One of its verses went:

The Church shall stand, the Queen shall reign,
In spite of the Fanatick,
And Whigs shall never vote out again,
A Wrightson and a Blackett

This was a period of triennial parliaments and at the 1713 election Blackett and
Wrightson were unopposed. The accession of George I led to yet another election,
and, although this time there was a Whig candidate, James Clavering, Blackett and
Wrightson won comfortably.

Sir William Blackett was well known as a Jacobite sympathizer. There were many such
among the gentry of Northumberland and Durham, and the merchants of Newcastle,
while the Bishop of Durham, Nathaniel Crewe, was a supporter of the Stuarts. Tories

and Jacobites were by no means synonymous. Most Tories were uneasy about the events of 1688, but many, perhaps most, did not wish to see a Catholic on the throne. Nor must it be assumed that all Catholics were fervent Jacobites, though most were sympathizers. Catholic landowners suffered some civil disabilities but were integrated into county society and could live relatively prosperous lives; only a minority felt sufficiently strongly to risk lives and property for the Stuart cause. There was, nevertheless, a strong body of elite opinion, and a well of sympathy in popular opinion in the north, that favoured a Stuart restoration. That it was not easy to turn sympathizers into active rebels, without good evidence that rebellion would succeed, was to be demonstrated in 1715.

The nature of Sir William Blackett's Jacobitism is unclear. Was he always a serious plotter, or did he, like so many, enjoy raising his glass to the 'king over the water', and bluster his dislike for the Whigs and the Hanoverians, only to find, with his hangovers, that he had committed himself more than he would have wished? Certainly there is good evidence that he did commit himself to a rising in 1715, a rising that was originally to be centred on the north and to be accompanied by the landing of French troops and Jacobites from France on the Northumberland coast. Blackett's role was to ensure the delivery of Newcastle into Jacobite hands, for his influence in the town and particularly amongst its keelmen was accounted crucial. In the event, however, plans were changed and went awry. The main thrust of the rebellion was to come from the south west and, like the French landings, did not happen. A reasonable plan with a chance of success turned into a desperate venture.

Jacobite plotting was ever leaky, and there were hard and alert men watching.

William Cotesworth, a man who had risen from a tallow chandler's shop in Gateshead to become the lord of the manor of Gateshead and Whickham, and a major player in the north east's coal trade, was one. 'Black William' – the nickname was not affectionate – was the eyes and ears of Henry Liddell, the brain of the important Whig family the Liddells of Ravensworth Castle, who at this time was based in London.

The flag of James III was hoisted in Braemar early in September, but the English Jacobites awaited the landing of the Pretender. Nevertheless, before the rising in the north east of England took place, warrants were out for the arrest of the leading conspirators such as Forster, Derwentwater and Widdrington, and among them, Sir William Blackett.

Henry Liddell wrote to William Cotesworth on October 10, telling him to be careful to ensure that arms were not smuggled into Newcastle under loads of straw, 'if att this time itt be in the hands of friends', and went on:

Pray how stand your keelmen affected? This afternoon I see a letter which says that tis suspected a certain bar[onet, Blackett] *was amongst them, but I can't imagine a man off his noble fortune would run a risque more than probable off loosing all.*[14]

Blackett had indeed decided not to join the rebellion. According to some older authorities, he narrowly escaped arrest in Yorkshire on 3 October and then turned up at Newby Hall in Yorkshire, the house of his uncle, Sir Edward Blackett, on 19 October. According to Hodgson, Sir Edward, in a statement clearly aimed to clear his nephew and himself of suspicion, said:

Sir William told me he came that day from Newcastle, and that he had been forced to fly from Wallington, having been pursued by Mr Forster and a great many Northumbrian gentlemen who were then in arms against king George; and he told me he believed their design was to have forced him to join them, and that he was much pursued by the King's forces who suspected him to be in the rebels' interest... I advised him to go to London as thinking it the most secure place and where he might have an opportunity of accommodating things with the Court.[15]

A recent account by Leo Gooch has Sir William learning that the warrant for his arrest was put out while he was staying with Sir Edward, but then making his way back to Wallington and hiding out there under surveillance, with the authorities hesitating to arrest him. In late October, Blackett, by this account, journeyed to Yorkshire, where he stayed with his 'younger brother' (in fact his brother-in-law) Sir Walter Calverley, to whom the same statement attributed by Hodgson to Sir Edward Blackett is also attributed.[16]

Whatever Blackett's exact movements, or the extent of his involvement in the rising, he was in great danger. It was generally believed that he was one of the inner circle of conspirators and had deserted the rebellion only at the last moment. This was probably close to the truth, though it has to be remembered that those watchful Hanoverians, Cotesworth and Liddell, were uncertain as to the extent of his involvement:

As to Sir W[illiam Blackett] *I was over and above cautious. I was pumped by severall to know my opinion how far he was ingaged; my answer was that gentlem*[an] *was in possession of too plentiful a fortune I thought than to ingage himself.*[17]

It may well have been also that, aware of the number of Northumberland gentry who were cautious Jacobites, and unsure of Newcastle's loyalty to the Hanoverian succession, Cotesworth, Liddell, John Johnson (High Sheriff of Northumberland in 1715) and other leading Hanoverians preferred not to attempt to arrest Blackett for fear of pushing him into declaring his Jacobite loyalties. In the event Sir William got away with it. He made his way to court and kissed hands. He wasn't popular with anybody, for he seemed a traitor to the Hanoverians and Jacobites alike, but his head and his fortune were intact. He paid the modest price of a temporary loss of popularity, and was for a while shunned by Newcastle and county worthies. He lost the mayoral election in 1717, but was elected in 1718 after producing credentials of his loyalty from the government, and he retained his parliamentary seat until his death in 1728.

Much of his erstwhile popularity was regained because he was a free-spending man. He gave generously to charity and to public causes, clothing all the boys at St Andrew's Charity School, founded by his father, and repairing the altar at Hexham Abbey. At election times he entertained the electors of Newcastle in an open-handed way, while on the occasion of his marriage to Lady Barbara Villiers he provided enough free alcoholic drink to enable the citizens of Newcastle and much of the county to be drunk for several days. There were banquets, bonfires and bell-ringing. An amazing scene was witnessed on Shafto Crags, where the basin in the rock at its highest point, known as the Devil's Punchbowl, was deemed too small for a drinking bowl to mark the festivities. It was enlarged before being filled for the celebratory and soon befuddled throng, who danced to the music of a Northumbrian piper.

The bottles stood all ranked in a line,
The product of the barley and the vine.
Healths to Sir William and his spouse did pass,
And at each health they briskly broke a glass.
And ev'ry time they drink a health they rise,
And with huzzas they pierce the vaulted skies.[18]

Portrait of Lady Barbara Blackett, née Villiers, who married Sir William Blackett in 1725. *Wallington, The Trevelyan Collection (The National Trust) Derrick E. Witty.*

Another local poet exalted the beauty of Lady Barbara in terms not quite appropriate for a description of the bride of the lord of the manor:

Her breasts so pure and white, you would not know
But for their clearness, from two mounts of snow.[19]

At Hexham the bellringers were so enthusiastic that they broke the great 'fray' bell of St Mary's Church.

Despite being so well celebrated, the marriage was childless and, with Sir William's death in 1728, the baronetcy he had inherited from his father was to die out. William had, however, arranged for an heir to his considerable estates. He had not married until the age of thirty-six, but he had fathered a son and daughter with Elizabeth Ord of West Ord, County Durham, and he left all his estates to his daughter, another Elizabeth, provided she married Walter Calverley, son of his brother-in-law, Sir Walter Calverley, within twelve months, and provided that Walter took the name of Blackett. This was a pretty good offer, for Sir William's

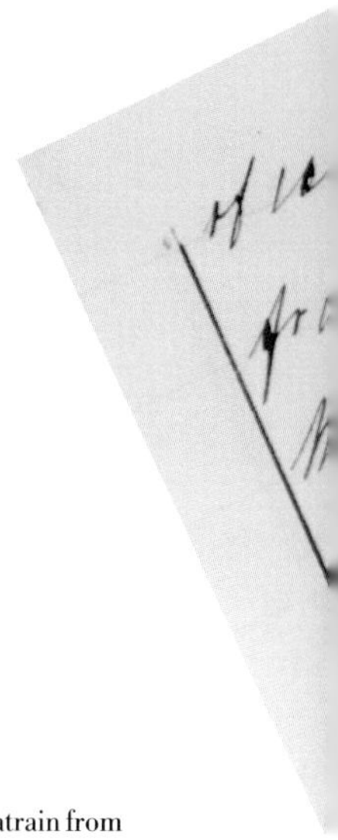

The Wallington quatrain from Lady Alethea's book.

estates were extensive and valuable, even if encumbered by debts of £77,000. It was accepted.

The Blacketts' motto is 'Nous travaillerons en l'esperance', and from generation to generation they have tended to be hopeful and optimistic. Even when they were merchants, they did not combine their facility for making money with caution about spending it, and their attitude towards expenditure and debt rapidly acquired an aristocratic style. Their extravagance brought political rewards and public approval; after all, what is the point of the very rich if they don't build great houses, give splendid parties or contribute generously to worthy causes? Sir William was, however, on the scale of wealth-creation and expenditure decidedly unbalanced towards the latter. He spent freely with little thought for the morrow and indulged himself with every fashionable whim. It was, for instance, fashionable in the eighteenth century to have a black servant, but Sir William went one better and, in the last year of his life, took on an indentured native American servant. My use of the term 'native American' as opposed to 'Red Indian' is not inspired by twenty-first-century political correctness, but follows the language of the 'Bond for Life':

I Galba, a Native of America ...freely and voluntarily bind myself unto the said Sir William Blackett...to serve ...him during the course of my natural life in such capacity and in such manner as he ...shall appoint or command.[20]

It is not known whether Galba remained at Wallington after William's death.

Although the size of Sir William's debts was largely the result of his own extravagance,

…ial songs, and many traditions, …
…at happened here after a hard day's chase.
…y to Wallington" is an old and favourite air in the
…bourhood.

"Harnham was headless, Bradford breadless
Shaftoe pick at the craw
Capheaton was a wee bonny place
But Wallington banged them a'."

This old hospitality of the house could not however, be supported, after a frequent residence in London, and the profligate habits of the court of Charles II, began to make their demands upon the rental of the estate, and it is not improbable that the same cause which led to the sale of the property of this once powerful family, had also a hand in leading the last of its owners to his sad end. In changing owners, however the place had none of its former magnificence abated. An old rhymster, alluding to the festal habits of the place, and the rebuilding of it, says.

"The name of Wallington old songsters praise
The Phoenix* from her ashes Blackett raise."

* alluding to the Fenwick crest, which is a pun upon the name.

he himself had been left debts by his father, who had died owing £7600 to Thomas Davidson, a Newcastle merchant, and Elizabeth Davidson, a spinster of Middlesex. The trouble was that William didn't pay off this debt until 1724, when he did so after taking out a mammoth £65,000 mortgage on a great part of the estate to a London banker, in the same month as he took out another mortgage held by Lancelot Allgood of Hexham, his agent.[21]

True to form Sir William raised money for his own funeral by ordering in his will that his fourth part of the Winlaton estate be sold or mortgaged to pay his debts, legacies and funeral expenses. Like his father's, his was a grand funeral. The chief mourners in St Nicholas's Church were headed by his heir, Walter Calverley.

Portrait of Sir Walter Calverley Blackett (1708–77) by Sir Joshua Reynolds.
Wallington, The Trevelyan Collection (The National Trust) Derrick E. Witty.

SIR WALTER CALVERLEY BLACKETT 1708–1777

Welford referred to Sir Walter Blackett as King of Newcastle, and indeed he was even more wealthy and influential than the William Blacketts who preceded him.

Walter Calverley married Elizabeth Ord on 29 August 1729 and by a private Act of Parliament took the name Blackett in 1734. Such a change of name was in accordance, as was the marriage, with the conditions for his inheritance, and was a not unusual stratagem in a period that has been described as one of 'demographic crisis' for aristocracy and gentry, for maintaining the association of name and property in the absence of heirs in the direct line. Walter Calverley was, in his own right, heir to his father's baronetcy and to the valuable Yorkshire estates of Esholt, Calverley and Horsforth.

He moved easily and swiftly into the traditional Blackett positions in Newcastle. He was made a Freeman and then an Alderman and, a few months after taking the name of

SIR WALTER BLACKETT
SIR JOSHUA REYNOLDS

Blackett, he was elected MP in 1734. In 1735 he was mayor and was to hold that office again in 1748, 1756, 1764 and 1771.

The Blackett inheritance, though considerable, was in disarray because of the late Sir William's extravagance. Sir Walter managed his estates well, and in his time the lead mines and mills moved back into a profitable condition. He was, perhaps, fortunate, in that profits from lead mining seem to have increased generally in the 1730s. He inherited the capable managers of his estates, Lancelot Allgood and Joseph Richmond, and was later to employ his equally capable relative John Erasmus Blackett. By 1734, Richmond was able to write that 'the debts owing at Sir William's death to the mines and mills, on simple contracts, his funeral expenses and also a year's interest then behind have all been repaid and discharged after the personal estate he left, and the profits arising between his death and your marriage'. He went on to point out that the profits of the estate were almost solely due to the lead mines, which had made £5500 a year for the last three years. [22]

His uncle's extravagance had been so great, however, that Wallington itself was mortgaged, and it was not until 1750 that he acquired the full title, when he bought it along with Fallowlees, Sweethope and Hawick, at a sale ordered by the Court of Chancery to settle Sir William's debts for £70,000. He also bought Longwitton from the Swinburnes and bought out the Lilburns' share of the Kenton estate, which latter he soon sold in its entirety. These transactions were paid for by the sale of the Yorkshire estates he had inherited from his father in 1749. Sir William's mortgages cast a long shadow (the Trevelyans were still paying off some of them in the nineteenth century), but Sir Walter was now secure and was truly Sir Walter Calverley Blackett Bt. of Wallington and Hexham Priory.

He worked hard for Newcastle's interests and was a notable philanthropist. As an MP he introduced a bill for the lighting and watch-keeping of the town which, after dark, was a dangerous place. The bill passed its second reading but got no further. During his first term as mayor, he was responsible for the erection of the building to the south of St Nicholas's Church, to provide for a vestry with accommodation on the first floor for the old church library. Sir Walter provided a salary of £25 a year for the librarian. He was a patron of the infirmary and in 1758 gave £1000 to it as well as £1200 to help found a hospital for six poor unmarried burgesses and £200 to the erection of a lunatic asylum. As well as being generous to Newcastle charities, Sir Walter was liberal in times of hardship, such as the severe winter of 1739 when the Tyne froze over and, with all trade at a stop, there was considerable distress.

Like his uncle, Sir Walter was a Tory. The events of 1715 had weakened the Tory hold on Newcastle, and Sir William's later electoral victories had not been easy. He had held his seat in 1722 but had come second to the Whig, William Carr. Though in 1727 he and another Tory, Nicholas Fenwick, had won, the losing Whig, Carr, had petitioned Parliament, alleging bribery and menace, and took the seat when Sir William died. Sir Walter and Nicholas Fenwick made a formidable partnership, however, and they topped the polls in 1734 and 1741. The political divide was at its widest in 1741, when Blackett and Fenwick emphasized their opposition to the Whig or Court Party, as represented by William Carr and the prominent merchant Matthew Ridley, and stood for not only the Tory but the Country Party.

On Boxing Day 1740, Ridley's supporters marched through the town with colours and music and a background noise of bells and gunfire, while on New Year's Day Blackett and Fenwick organized a similar march, after which the crowd of over a

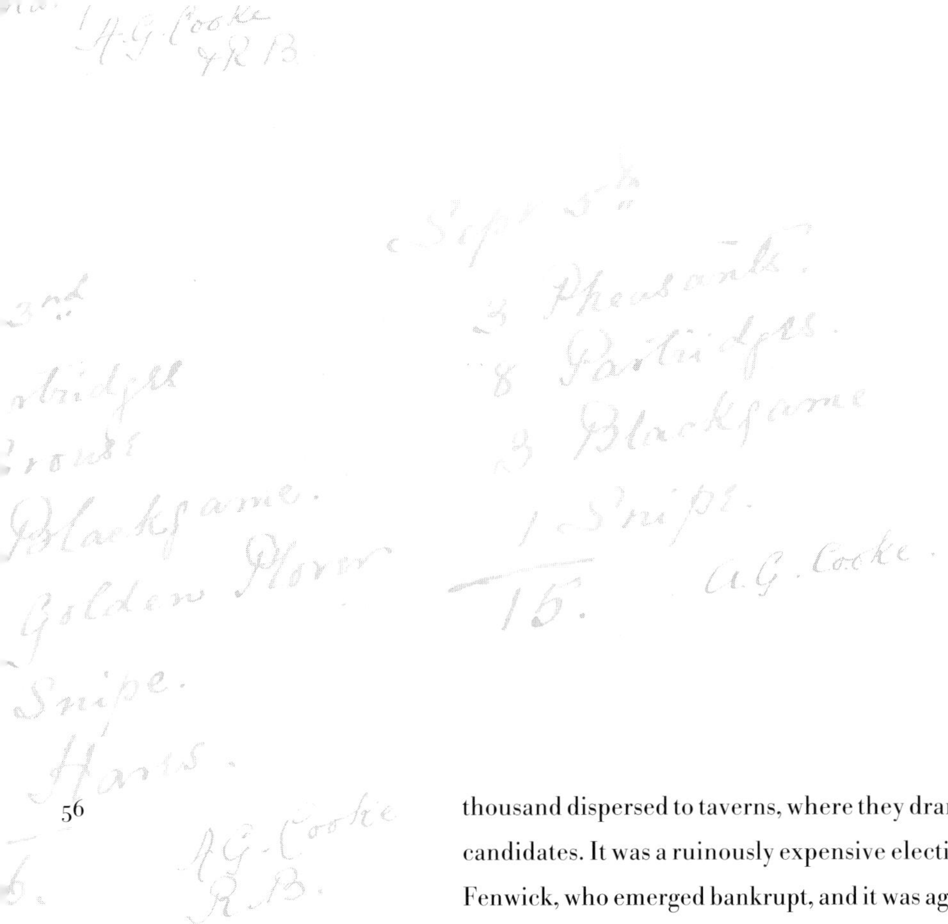

thousand dispersed to taverns, where they drank the health of the hospitable Tory candidates. It was a ruinously expensive election for all concerned, literally so for Fenwick, who emerged bankrupt, and it was again followed by an attempt to unseat the victors by petition to parliament. Blackett's expenses amounted to £6319. Two blue-and-white punchbowls at Wallington celebrate the electoral victory, and are inscribed 'Lett us drink success to Blackett and Fenwick'. Newcastle's electors had been given every opportunity to do just that.

Passions had cooled somewhat by 1747. This was in part because the town had remained united during the 1745 rebellion, with the local Tories exhibiting no taste for Jacobite adventures. Blackett had built at his own expense a fort, known as Cadger's Fort, on the old Salters' Way to protect the approach from Scotland, and entertained the Duke of Cumberland and his officers on their return after Culloden. Though Blackett remained opposed to the Court until the accession of George III, he increasingly portrayed himself as an independent member:

The only interest I stand upon you must know is the inclination and good will of my friends, for I aim at no other characteristics than that of an honest easy good neighbour who, when he must judge in politics and state affairs, will do it to the best of his capacity with the little light which generally falls to the share of a country gentleman. But I delight not in party, and have been a witness to, if not an actor in, the absurdity of it.[23]

The move towards an alliance between Ridley and Blackett probably owed much to the expense of the previous contest, and a wary recognition by Blackett and Ridley of each

other's strength and influence in the town. Blackett in particular was a formidable fighter of elections: 'attended often by above five hundred gentlemen tradesmen etc. some of whom had weight with almost every freeman'.[24] But elections cost a lot of money, so why not moderate party strife? This tacit alliance discomposed their more zealous supporters, but the business of Newcastle was essentially commerce: other candidates withdrew and Blackett and Ridley were unopposed. This electoral truce was to continue for decades with Blackett and Ridley being returned without opposition until 1774, when, eventually meeting opposition, they nevertheless topped the polls.

Sir Walter Blackett was a good businessman, a benevolent employer, a philanthropist and a man who spent extravagantly on his lifestyle and upon his politics. That this made him very popular is unsurprising, for almost everyone in Newcastle and on his estates in the Pennines and around Hexham benefited in some way from these traits. It is easy to sneer at the very rich when they are amiable, generous and philanthropic. That they had a right to be good-natured, considering their fortunate position, may be asserted, but the rich and fortunate are not always amiable or generous. Those with little historical sense of different times and mores can point to the short lives of those who worked in Blackett lead mines or smelting mills, or to what were, by early twenty-first-century standards, the inadequate housing and long, back-breaking hours of labour of the agricultural workers on Sir Walter's estates. Those who worked in his lead mines and upon his farms were, however, grateful for their employment and his paternal nature. He provided clergy and churches and schools and schoolmasters for those who worked for him, and you could not go far in the North Pennines or around

Hexham without seeing the name Blackett on some building erected for public use.

Rural Northumberland was, in the eighteenth century, changing rapidly. Peaceful after centuries of border disturbances, its agriculture was flourishing, just as in its south west corner lead mining was expanding. An improvement in communications was an essential part of the county's development, and Sir Walter was zealous in promoting new roads and improvements to old ones. He invested £500 in the road across country from Hexham to Alnmouth, paid towards the repair of the Elsdon turnpike and contributed £200 to the repair and completion of the road to Carlisle.

Once secure in his inheritance, he turned his attention to what became his principal residence for, if Anderson Place remained his town house and an important base for promoting his electoral and business interests in Newcastle, it was Wallington that he considered as his seat. His predecessors had probably regarded Wallington as the secondary residence, a shooting lodge and a place to entertain guests. As a later owner, Sir Charles Trevelyan, describes the house Sir Walter inherited:

There were neither corridors nor galleries nor passages within the walls of the original Wallington. The rooms in defiance of privacy, opened one into another round the entire circuit of the house, and the vast garrets in the roof, where county freeholders and Newcastle constituents slept the sleep of men who, in those all too inhospitable days, had been dining with their party leader, were not separated into cubicles by partitions of wood, or lath or plaster, but ran without a break over the spaces of nearly forty yards from angle to angle of the building.[25]

Sir Walter employed Daniel Garret as his architect, and the house was largely rebuilt over a period of more than twenty years, eventually retaining little but the basic layout of the house designed by Sir William fifty years earlier.

Instead of the main entrance being on the southside, it was moved to the east. The north side was rebuilt and the interior remodelled. An outstanding feature is the grassed stable yard, with its range of cottages and stables, which is approached by the Clock Tower Gate, topped by a cupola on nine Doric columns. Sir William's house had been built around a courtyard, and Garret reduced the size of this in order to install a corridor running around the house, thus doing away with the inconvenience of having to proceed room by room. A fine staircase, which becomes a double staircase after the first flight, was inserted on the south side of the quadrangle. Sir Walter's guests were entertained as liberally as had been those of the two Sir Williams, but they could be helped or carried upstairs more easily and would find more comfortable quarters in which to sleep after their libations.

As much care was devoted to the planning of the gardens and park as to the house itself. This was indeed an ambitious project, originally planned in 1740, with a new plan in 1750 and further innovations in the 1760s. The earlier landscaping involved the damming of streams to form ponds, the planting of the West Wood with its walks and arbours, and an enclosed garden to the east, now a wooded area, although the pond that it contained and the Portico House remain. The new kitchen garden, a walled garden about a third of a mile to the east of the house, is said to have been one of the improvements suggested by 'Capability' Brown. It was certainly an inspired concept: south-facing and with a small stream flowing through it, what had been a pleasant

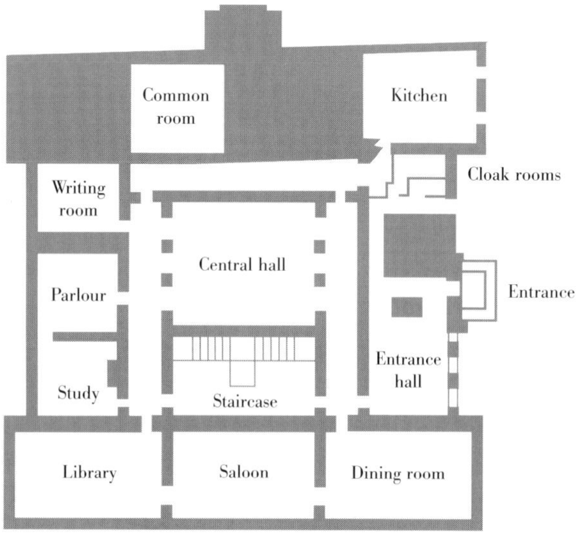

Floorplan of Wallington.

'The house is a quadrangle of two stories, built around a small court (which court Sir Walter Trevelyan by throwing a roof over it converted into a central hall, and the passages connecting the rooms in the upper and lower storeys were opened into it, in the form of arcades) and having arched cellars on three sides. The north and south front measure 119 feet, the east and west 114. Sir William Blackett added the cornice round it, rebuilt the south front, made a new staircase and carried covered passages around the whole internal area, besides embellishing the walls and ceiling of the dining room, saloon, and drawing room, with good designs in stucco work, and elegant marble chimney pieces. He also built the clock house, from a design of Payne.' (Lady Alethea's book)

Lead sculptures from Holland, formerly in the garden at Anderson Place, now lining the terrace of the walled garden at Wallington.

dell became a garden both elegant and comfortable, with its walls, brickwork terraces, flower beds and fruit trees. The lead figures imported from Holland that line the terrace had previously stood in the gardens of Anderson Place.

Eighteenth-century landowners were cavalier with public roads or villages that detracted from their privacy or spoiled the view. Sir Walter had the hamlet to the north of Wallington demolished, but rehoused the inhabitants in the planned village of Cambo. It is an attractive village and no doubt its resettled inhabitants were grateful. The public road running close to the house was another matter. The solution was to move it from the west to the east side of the house so that it looked like a private drive, and to give it a grand entrance in the form of the wonderful Palladian bridge across the Wansbeck. In addition, the road was cleverly lowered between the bridge and the house, so that the travellers would not intrude into the view or be able to gaze at the house from close quarters.

The countryside around Wallington still bears his mark. Wealthy eighteenth-century gentry were not content simply to improve or build their houses and set out their gardens, but rather aspired to sculpt the landscape they viewed from their windows, and to improve and edify the countryside for miles around. Economic interest came together with elevated taste, often influenced by paintings of Italian scenes. It was the former that led to enclosures and a more scientific approach to farming, as Northumberland moved towards becoming a county associated with innovation and prosperity. Sir Walter encouraged the improvement of farms, and the enclosure of the land and the planting of fine hedges of whitethorn. He built stone cottages for farm-labourers, replacing what had often been thatched dwellings, while

the roads on his own estate were described by Arthur Young as 'a piece of magnificence'. Yet the changes he made were not confined to the utilitarian, but were also inspired by an aesthetic sensibility. Like so many of his contemporaries, Sir Walter planted trees: the beeches to the north, west and east of Wallington, and some of the first larches to be planted in Britain. Sharing the contemporary taste for constructing points of interest, he delighted in enlivening the scenery with lakes, woods and 'eye-catchers', and creating Rothley Lake. His tastes were far from confined to the classical mainstream . At Rothley Crags he erected an ambitious eye-catcher, a mock ruined castle, and surrounded it with all sorts of exotica: whale bones, and effigies and heads taken from the gates to the City of London, then being demolished. At Wallington itself visitors are today greeted by the heads of griffins that adorned first Bishopsgate and then Rothley Crags. The 'castle' on Rothley Crags was only part of the extensive pleasure ground with an artificial lake that Sir Walter and 'Capability' Brown, born at nearby Kirkharle, created in what had been a deer park.

Sir Walter took his responsibilities as lord of the manor of Hexham as seriously as those that came with his Newcastle offices. He often stayed at his Hexham house, Prior's House, and walks were laid and trees planted by Sir Walter in the grounds close to the abbey, and the inhabitants of the town were permitted to walk in them. He also built the colonnaded *piazza* in the Market Square.

William Hutchinson, in his *A View of the County of Northumberland* published in 1778, commented on Sir Walter's charitable activities in Hexham:

Sir Walter Calverley Blackett gave several valuable gifts for the augmentation of the living; and many charities have been left for the relief of the poor. It is a doubt with me, whether these donations to the poor do not induce indigent and impotent persons to crowd a town, and in effect encourage idleness.[26]

Hutchinson's rather hard-headed opinion was not shared by most Northumbrians. The tribute to Sir Walter by John Hodgson may seem overdone to modern eyes, but it probably reflected the view of him in the decades after his death:

His splendour was the power that kept many thousand hands in motion – that cheered and comforted the feeble and the destitute... In his equipage and establishment there was a decent grandeur; in hospitality and household affairs sumptuousness and regularity. His gallantry is often mentioned and his manners are said to have been dignified.[27]

When he was about forty, he was described by the Reverend Alexander Carlyle as 'a very genteel looking man...who had not been happy with his lady'. According to Carlyle, he was in love with his cousin when they married but 'she did not care for him. By report she was of superior understanding to him for he was not a man of remarkable parts, but strong in friendships, liberality and public spirit...'[28]

Despite the dignified manner there was something of the robust country squire about Sir Walter. Edward Grierson commented that the Reynolds portrait of

> *...this portly country squire in an old brown suit and shovel hat, attended by his dog, perfectly displays the mixture of the rustic and the grandiose that marked the English gentry at the high tide of their fortunes.*[29]

His father, it has been asserted, was the model for Addison's Sir Roger de Coverley. Sir Walter cared little for status conferred by birth, asserting that a man held his honour and reputation in his own hands. Like many a Northumberland squire, he enjoyed mixing with farmers and ordinary country people, and was fond of shooting and fishing; his favourite companions were probably his much-loved dogs. He had little in the way of intellectual interests and was a restless man who was bored indoors, though he filled his house with guests. We can assume that he had a hearty sexual appetite, which largely found its outlet in the arms of servants and country women rather than with ladies of rank. He was described when aged about sixty as

> *...of a strong robust Make, and was call'd a handsome Man. He has been greatly addicted to Women but his Amours have been chiefly among Servant Maids & Women of that Class.*[30]

He certainly left a large number of annuities in his will to female servants and women in the neighbourhood and nearby towns, but then he was a generous man. An anonymous memorialist said of him: 'He had most of the virtues that cause a man to be beloved, and a large assortment of frailties which in those far from Puritanical days, told for rather than against his personal popularity'.[31]

After years of being unopposed Blackett and Ridley had to face fierce opposition at the election of 1774. Sir Walter had offended some of the freemen by taking the unpopular side in the dispute over the Town Moor between the freemen and the town magistrates, a dispute that ended in victory for the burgesses. The town was also drawn into the national agitation in the wake of the Wilkes affairs and candidates all over the country were asked to subscribe to the radical Wilkite manifesto. Blackett and Ridley both refused to subscribe to it and were opposed by Sir Francis Delaval and the Hon. Constantine John Phipps. Despite the ferocity of the contest the sitting members won comfortably, but Sir Walter was much hurt by the opposition to him, especially when it was found amongst those he had done so much to help. He nevertheless stuck to his political principles, and when, in the following year, 1210 freemen signed a petition against the war with the American colonists, both Sir Walter and Matthew Ridley refused to present it.

For much of his political career he had opposed the establishment and had been seen as 'The patriot, the opposer of the court and the father of the poor'. His opposition, however, had been to a Whig hegemony rather than being a mere fractious opposition to central government as such. After George III's succession he was himself of the Court Party. If this brought him some unpopularity with erstwhile supporters, it seemed likely to lead to a peerage, and this was confidently expected at the time of his death in London in 1777.

Despite having made Wallington his home, he was buried at his native Calverley. He had no heir as his only child, a daughter, had died young. The entailed estates went to Thomas Wentworth, son of his aunt, Diana Blackett. She had married Sir

Overleaf:
Rothley Crags.

THE SHIP THAT CAME HOME

Pochard. foggy.
Golden Eye.

Teal.   Fine, little frost.
goosander.

Teal.
Mallards.

y hot

68

William Wentworth of Bretton Hall, Wakefield. They had five sons but, remarkably, none married. Sir Thomas (he inherited the Wentworth baronetcy) took the name of Blackett in accordance with the provisions of Sir Walter's will.

Sir Walter's nephew, the son of his sister, Julia, who had married Sir George Trevelyan of Nettlecombe in Somerset, inherited Wallington.[32] Sir John Trevelyan had already succeeded to his family's estates in 1757. The Trevelyans were to put down deep roots at Wallington and to establish a reputation, very different from that of the Blacketts, for plain living, intellectual pursuits and radical politics. This was, however, certainly not a description of Sir Walter's brother-in-law, Sir George, who ran through the family's money, made the vicar's daughter his mistress and had a bare-fisted fight with another west-country squire, Sir Thomas Acland. His son, Sir John, was a steadier character who had married an heiress to a considerable fortune, but even though he moved to Wallington and initially interested himself in Newcastle politics, paying the debts Sir Walter had incurred in fighting the 1774 election and then standing successfully himself in 1777, he then seems to have tired of life in the north and he moved back to Somerset. His younger brother, Walter, married the heiress to nearby Netherwitton Hall and settled there, establishing a second Northumberland Trevelyan dynasty.

Later baronets divided their time between the two estates of Wallington and Northumberland. It was only with the rather inappropriately named Sir Walter Calverley Trevelyan, an evangelical, a pacifist and a great promoter of temperance, that Wallington became the Trevelyans' main home. He and his wife, Pauline, a woman of literary and artistic interests and a friend of John Ruskin, were responsible for the next significant alteration to Wallington. The house had been designed with a central courtyard, but in 1853–54 this was roofed in. A series of columns formed a balustrade around what now became a hall, and between 1864 and 1867 panels depicting great events in Northumberland's history were painted by William Bell Scott, an associate of the Pre-Raphaelites. Artistic taste and high-mindedness did not coexist with comfort in the arrangements at Wallington, and Augustus Hare, that indefatigable Victorian traveller, who stayed almost everywhere, recorded spartan living conditions, plain and meagre food, and an absence of alcohol. Sir Walter had no children, and on his death the estates were divided. Wallington went to a cousin, Sir Charles Edward Trevelyan, a baronet in his own right, and Nettlecombe to the heir to the original Trevelyan baronetcy, Sir Alfred Trevelyan.

The death of Sir Walter Blackett resulted in the end of the Blackett connection with that 'princely mansion', the Newe House. The Trevelyans offered to sell it to the Corporation of Newcastle. The corporation, surprisingly in view of its potential, declined to purchase the house, largely because, despite its usually cautious attitude towards public expenditure, it was already engaged in building Mosley Street and Dean Street, so the development of Newcastle's prime site was put off for another half-century. It was sold to Major Anderson, an 'opulent builder', for £10,000 in 1782. He converted the house into three residences, and his son renamed it Anderson Place. Thomas Anderson inherited the estate on his uncle's death in 1831 and decided to sell it. Richard Grainger, with the support of the Town Clerk, John Clayton, emerged as the most serious contender for the house and grounds, and in

Far left: The roofed-in central courtyard, showing sculpture bought and commissioned by Pauline Trevelyan: Thomas Woolner's *The Lord's Prayer* and Alexander Munro's *Paolo and Francesca*.
Wallington, The Trevelyan Collection (The National Trust) Derrick E. Witty.

Left: Grace Darling by William Bell Scott.
Wallington, The Trevelyan Collection (The National Trust) Derrick E. Witty.

1834 the Common Council of Newcastle accepted Grainger's development plans. Grainger and his associates paid £59,000 for the house and grounds, and Anderson Place, for so long Newcastle's premier house, was demolished.

The site became the key part of Richard Grainger's redevelopment of the city, with its network of wide streets and sophisticated buildings. The result was the magnificent Grey Street, the Grainger Market, and Clayton and Grainger Streets, an area now saluted by Newcastle City Council as Grainger Town, and which has justly been much celebrated. It is, nevertheless, interesting to ponder whether the plans that John Dobson – Newcastle's and the north east's most important architect – had for Anderson Place would have resulted in a development that would have been more verdant and equally successful, providing Newcastle with a magnificent civic centre. A recent study of John Dobson has described his plans for the site, which included:

… on the site of Anderson Place itself should be built a Mansion House with 'four handsome stone fronts, the north, south and west sides to rise from a bold terrace;

A tea party in the Central Hall, 1899. *The National Trust Photographic Library.*

and the latter to be ornamented with eight beautiful pillars. The east front to face Pilgrim Street, and to have a lofty grand portico, capable of admitting carriages.' With the sensitive eye of the landscape gardener, he proposed retaining the avenue of trees leading from Pilgrim Street to Anderson Place as part of the ceremonial approach to this new 'civic palace.'[33]

Sir Thomas Wentworth Blackett died in 1792 and left the Yorkshire estates and the greater part of the Blackett inheritance to Diana, the wife of Colonel Thomas Richard Beaumont. Diana was an illegitimate child of Sir Thomas. Alethea Blackett states that she was the daughter of Sir Thomas's lodge keeper at Bretton Park, herself the daughter of the gamekeeper. The unmarried Sir Thomas appears in fact to have had three daughters for, according to the *Gentleman's Magazine* (July 1792), two other daughters, Mrs Lee and Miss Louisa Wentworth, also benefited from his will, being left £3000 a year and substantial capital sums. A Captain Stackpole was later committed to prison after Colonel Beaumont began proceedings against him for marrying Louisa while she was still a ward of Chancery. Stackpole was, however, released so that he could rejoin his regiment. The *Newcastle Chronicle* pointed out that by the terms of Sir Thomas's will she would forfeit £10,000 for marrying before she was twenty-one, but would retain her £3000 per annum.[34]

Diana Beaumont, the chief beneficiary of her father's will, was not universally popular. Alethea Blackett, who had Yorkshire connections, local knowledge and, no doubt, prejudices, copied out the following depiction of Diana:

Bookplate designed by William Bell Scott, commissioned by Sir Walter Trevelyan as a birthday present for his wife, Pauline, in 1858. Lady Alethea also reproduces this in her book.

> *The chief potentate in our part of the West Riding at that time was Mrs Beaumont of Bretton known by the people throughout the country as Madame Beaumont…She eventually married Colonel Beaumont. But the Colonel drank and had to be placed in his butler's care, so there was nothing to interfere with Madame's rule. She was a wilful, purse-proud woman, very ambitious and very ostentatious.*[35]

The Beaumonts, whose Yorkshire estates included rich coal-mining land, thus added to them the Blackett estates in the Allen Valley with their profitable lead mines. Diana Beaumont rebuilt Priory House at Hexham, which had been badly damaged by a fire. Miss Mary Russell Mitford, the author, visited it in 1806 and wrote of 'the bad taste of this abominable modern house'.[36] Prior's House was, however, fire-prone and in 1817 and 1818 there were two fires, the last of which almost destroyed the house. It was rebuilt again on a reduced scale, but the

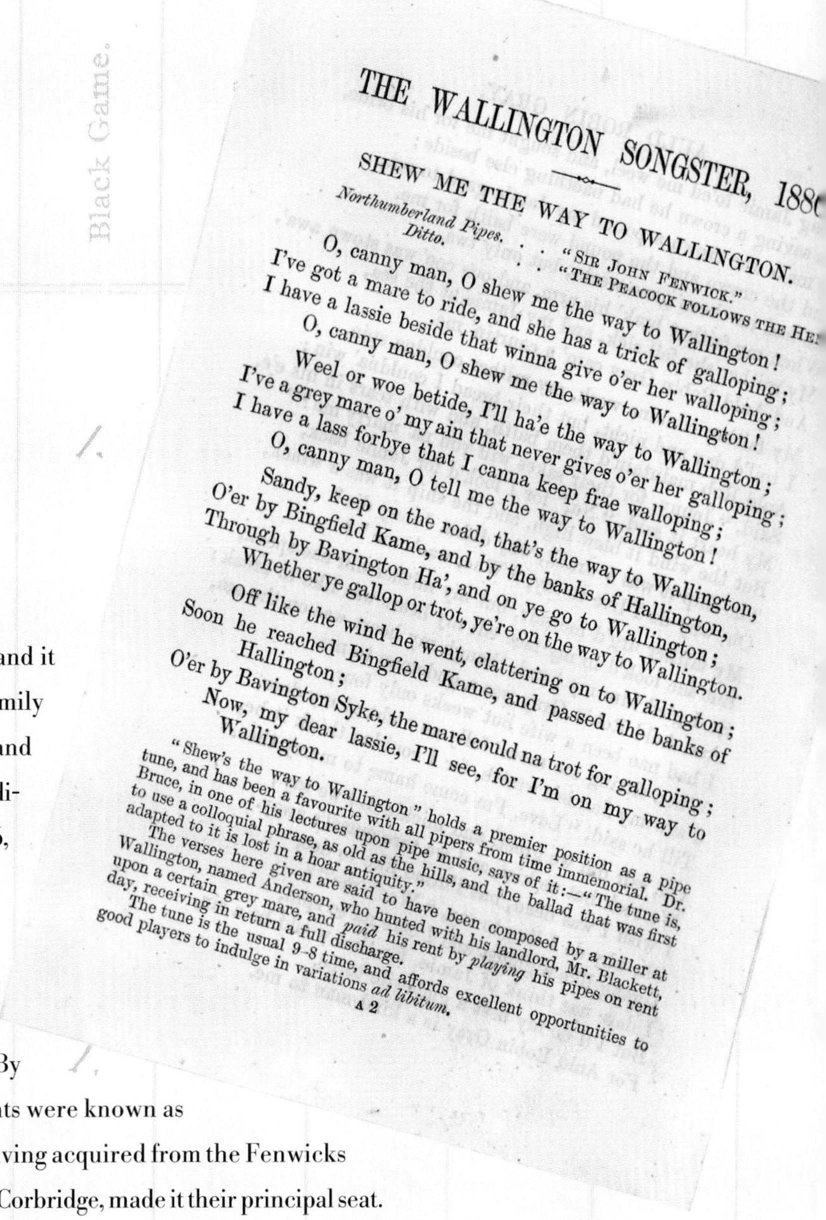

THE WALLINGTON SONGSTER, 188

SHEW ME THE WAY TO WALLINGTON.

Northumberland Pipes. . . "SIR JOHN FENWICK."
Ditto. . . "THE PEACOCK FOLLOWS THE HE

O, canny man, O shew me the way to Wallington!
I've got a mare to ride, and she has a trick of galloping;
I have a lassie beside that winna give o'er her walloping;
O, canny man, O shew me the way to Wallington!

Weel or woe betide, I'll ha'e the way to Wallington;
I've a grey mare o' my ain that never gives o'er her galloping;
I have a lass forbye that I canna keep frae walloping;
O, canny man, O tell me the way to Wallington!

Sandy, keep on the road, that's the way to Wallington,
O'er by Bingfield Kame, and by the banks of Hallington,
Through by Bavington Ha', and on ye go to Wallington,
Whether ye gallop or trot, ye're on the way to Wallington;

Off like the wind he went, clattering on to Wallington.
Soon he reached Bingfield Kame, and passed the banks of Hallington;
O'er by Bavington Syke, the mare could na trot for galloping;
Now, my dear lassie, I'll see, for I'm on my way to Wallington.

"Shew's the way to Wallington" holds a premier position as a pipe tune, and has been a favourite with all pipers from time immemorial. Dr. Bruce, in one of his lectures upon pipe music, says of it:—"The tune is, to use a colloquial phrase, as old as the hills, and the ballad that was first adapted to it is lost in a hoar antiquity."

The verses here given are said to have been composed by a miller at Wallington, named Anderson, who hunted with his landlord, Mr. Blackett, upon a certain grey mare, and *paid* his rent by *playing* his pipes on rent day, receiving in return a full discharge.

The tune is the usual 9–8 time, and affords excellent opportunities to good players to indulge in variations *ad libitum*.

A 2

The Wallington Songster (1880), as collected into Lady Alethea's book.

Beaumonts abandoned it as a family seat and it became a courthouse. By the 1820s the family had become established as Northumberland gentry. T.W. Beaumont became a Whig candidate in the Northumberland election of 1826, during which he fell out with the other Whig candidate, Lord Howick,[37] and fought a duel with Lord Lambton, one of Howick's supporters, on Bamburgh Sands. He was a strong supporter of the 1832 Reform Act. By the mid-nineteenth century the Beaumonts were known as the richest commoners in England and, having acquired from the Fenwicks Bywell Hall on the banks of the Tyne below Corbridge, made it their principal seat.

Thus came to an end the Blacketts of Wallington, despite two attempts to preserve the line by inheritances involving the adoption of the name Blackett, and two inheritances that secured the future of illegitimate daughters. Wallington remains, however, as a reminder of this dynasty whose enterprise and merchant wealth created a house and environs that, if not one of England's grandest stately homes, is one of the most attractive and charming.

2. THE BLACKETTS OF NEWBY HALL AND MATFEN

THE BLACKETTS OF MATFEN

Sir William Blackett (1621–1680) had, as we have seen, made 'two elder sons' by leaving considerable fortunes to William, upon whom Charles II bestowed a new baronetcy, and to Edward, who inherited his father's baronetcy in 1680. Edward first received estates rich in lead and coal as a marriage settlement from his father in 1674, and these landholdings were increased when he inherited another share of his father's wealth with the baronetcy.

Left: Portrait of Sir Edward Blackett, 2nd Bt. (*d.*1718).

Below: Photograph of Willimoteswick, *c.*1880, from Lady Alethea's book.

It is usually assumed that Edward retired from merchant life in Newcastle at the time of his first marriage to Mary, heiress to her father, Thomas Norton of Langthorne in Yorkshire. Certainly he moved from his Northumberland seat, Willimoteswick, to Langthorne on Thomas Norton's death. Throughout his life, however, he appears to have maintained an interest in business in Newcastle and, however nominal his supervision of apprentices may have been, we find apprentice Hostmen being indentured to him in 1702 and 1711.[38]

A long-established means of augmenting wealth was advantageous marriage, and, after the deaths of both his first wife and their son, Edward remarried. The bride was another Mary and

Portrait of Diana, 3rd wife of Sir Edward Blackett 2nd Bt., formerly Diana, Lady Delaval.

another heiress. Mary Yorke was the daughter of the deceased Sir John Yorke of Gouldthwaite (sometimes referred to as 'of Richmond'), Yorkshire, and, after a prolonged dispute over the marriage settlement with the bride's doughty mother, Edward married her in 1676.

Shortly after his second marriage, Edward bought the manor of Newby,[39] near Ripon in North Yorkshire. With the estate came a substantial Elizabethan house, which the new owner replaced with a magnificent residence built during the 1690s. It has been claimed that Sir Christopher Wren advised on the site and plan of the house and it certainly is in the style of Wren, though the architect was probably John Etty. Sir Edward devoted as much attention to the grounds and gardens as to the house and, indeed, it is clear that the terrace and gardens were designed to complement the house, following the same symmetry and proportions. He employed Peter Aram, who was among the leading gardeners of the day and had learned from George London and Henry Wise, those 'Heroick Poets' of gardening. The planning and development of the gardens were probably something of a team effort, with Aram realizing and interpreting the wishes of Sir Edward, and the indefatigable George London frequently visiting Newby to supervise the work of his student. We can assess the importance that Sir Edward attached to gardening from the fact that the gardener's wages were higher than those of any other member of the domestic staff. Aram was busy designing and planting at the same time as the new house was being built.[40] The result was the magnificent country house of Newby Hall.

Celia Fiennes visited Newby Hall in 1697, shortly after it was built. She describes it as

Above: The west front of Newby Hall, painted in the early eighteenth century. Artist unknown. *Reproduced by kind permission of Mr Richard Compton, Newby Hall.*

Right: Engraving of Newby Hall by Jan Kip.

> *... a fine place of Sir Edward Blackets, it looks finely in the approach in the midst of a good parke and a river runns just by it, it stands in the middle and has two large Gardens on each side... His house is built with brick and coyn'd with stone, with a flatte roof leaded, with Railes and Barristers, and a large Cupelow in the middle...*[40]

At the time of Celia Fiennes's visit, the house was in mourning for Sir Edward's second wife, who had borne him twelve children, six boys and six girls, before her death in 1696.

Sir Edward's interest seems to have oscillated between his Northumberland and Yorkshire estates. In his younger days he was an Alderman and a Mayor of Newcastle and a Sheriff of Northumberland, but he then became MP for Ripon in 1689. In 1698, after his second wife's death, he became MP for Northumberland. He was a moderate Tory, unlike his brother Sir William, who became a Whig. If he did not share his brother's enthusiasm for the Glorious Revolution, he was not a Jacobite. In 1715, though, as we have seen, he came under suspicion when he harboured his nephew, Sir William.

Like many of his family, he lived well, and was hospitable and inclined to extravagance. He had a house in York and a London residence in Dartmouth Street, in addition to Willimoteswick and Newby Hall. Even the profits from lead and coal couldn't quite support this lifestyle; the building of Newby Hall was supposed to have cost £35,000. By 1697 he had sold his first wife's manor of Langthorne and taken out a mortgage on Newby, while he frequently complained to his cousin John Blackett of Wylam and his agent James Meaburne, who looked after his mining interests, about the low price of lead.[42]

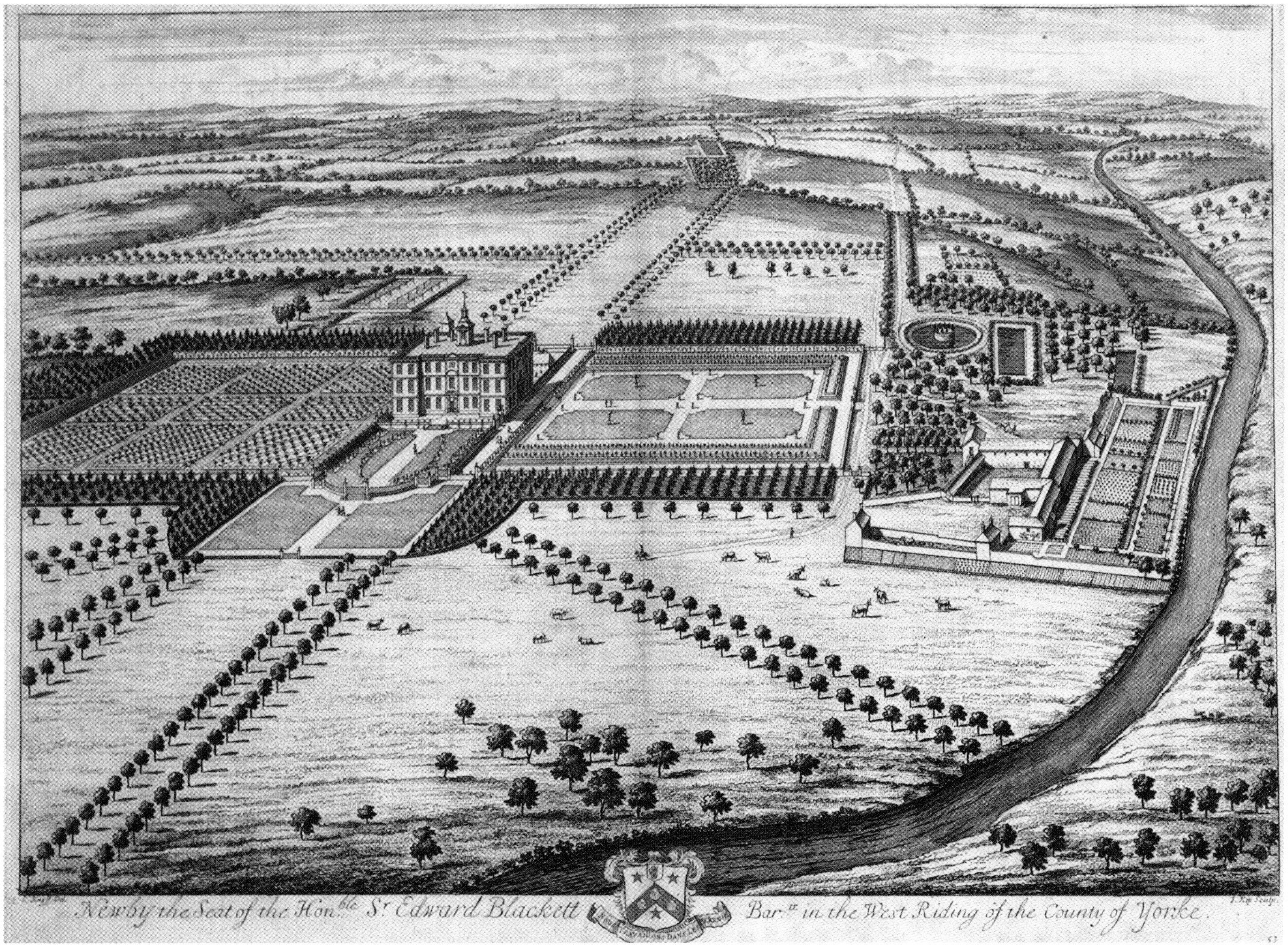
Newby the Seat of the Hon.ble Sr Edward Blackett Bar.tt in the West Riding of the County of Yorke.

Afternoon only.
M. Liddell came out
at lunch time. Showery,
3 snipe on Thornham Hill
on the way over.

A third marriage may have suggested itself as a means of augmenting his fortune. In 1699 Sir Edward was married again, this time to Diana, Lady Delaval, widow of Sir Ralph Delaval of Seaton Delaval. Two months later his eldest son, William, married Diana's thirteen-year-old daughter, another Diana.

Most marriages in this period had a financial dimension, but one can perceive Sir Edward's marriage to Diana, Lady Delaval, and William's subsequent marriage to her daughter as a pretty cold-blooded transaction. Sir Ralph Delaval had been something of an industrial entrepreneur, who had made the harbour that became Seaton Sluice suitable for colliers to take on cargoes of coal from his collieries. According to Francis Askham:

Afternoon

When Sir Ralph died, his cousin Sir John, who inherited the estates, seemed to lack interest in the coal industry, and was heavily in debt to a Sir Edward Blackett, a wealthy man and a pretty sharp one. Sir Edward Blackett married Sir Ralph's widow, who had a thirteen-year-old daughter with a tidy fortune of £8,000 to whom Sir Edward married his weakling son. This money was not paid over and Sir John would have appeared to have taken on this debt with the estates. The son died, and Sir Edward demanded the £8000 which together with interest had increased to £14,000 odd.[43]

With Sir John's refusal to pay up, the case went to the Court of Chancery, and Sir Edward obtained an order for the sale of the manor of Seaton. Luckily for the Delavals, a scion of a cadet branch of the family, George Delaval, had flourished in his naval

Seaton Delaval Hall.

career and was not only an admiral but also flush with prize money. After long negotiations with Blackett, Admiral Delaval paid off the debt, bought the estate and within a short time had employed Sir John Vanbrugh to design Seaton Delaval Hall.

The marriage of the young William Blackett to Diana Delaval made for a complex web of kinship for, although there was no blood relationship, she was Sir Edward's daughter-in-law and his stepdaughter, and he was his bride's stepbrother. Both William and Diana died before Sir Edward but they had a daughter, another Diana. To his credit Sir Edward was fond of the child and looked after her well enough, sending her to be brought up with her mother's cousin, the Earl of Warrington, who had a daughter of her own age.

He had, of course, a brood of children by his second wife, and his interest in them combined fondness and great care for their education with ambitions for their suitable marriages. He had a delicate sense as to the propriety of partners for his children and was outraged when one daughter, Anne, eloped with an attorney from Ripon. He quashed a potential marriage between his son Edward, who was now his heir, and Jane Saville, even though he was friendly with her father, but was quite content when she married one of his younger sons, Christopher.[44] The third son, John, married Patience, the daughter of Henry Wise, co-owner with George London of the Brompton Park nursery garden in Kensington. Whether it was Sir Edward's enthusiasm for gardening that allowed him to agree to this match, or the fact that Wise had made a fortune estimated at more than £100,000 from his gardening enterprise, is debatable.

After William's death in 1714 Edward, the second son, became the heir. The father had supported him in a naval career, using his influence with his neighbour, John Aislabie of Studley Royal, who was then Lord of the Admiralty,[45] to get him a captain's commission and command of a ship. He then, rather inappropriately, used his influence again to get the ship, *The Phoenix*, sent home, probably because of the death of William. Sir Edward's best-laid plans had gone awry. The heir, William, was dead and now Edward was the heir and had to leave the navy promptly. He married Mary, the daughter of the Reverend Thomas Jekyll and the widow of Nicholas Roberts, a merchant.

Sir Edward died in 1718 and was buried in Ripon Cathedral, beneath a full-length representation of himself lying between two ladies in mournful attitudes. Presumably images of all three wives would have rather crowded the assemblage. Things had not gone smoothly in his last years. Perhaps Sir Edward disapproved of his second son's marriage to the widow of a merchant. At any rate, he seems to have fallen out with his heir and he appointed his third son, John, to be his sole executor. By this time Sir Edward's affairs were in disarray and there were debts and liabilities amounting to £13,365. The will was disputed, but it was John who continued to live in Newby Hall, while the new Sir Edward, 3rd Bt. (1683–1756), moved to Northumberland.

The third baronet, who assumed the title in 1718, inherited considerable and profitable estates in Northumberland to the west of Hexham, which included the attractive

Photograph from Lady Alethea's book of the tomb of Sir Edward Blackett in Ripon Cathedral.

but quite simple house of Willimoteswick, the ancestral home of the Ridley family and one of the finest examples of a fortified manor in Northumberland. The house he inhabited was, however, Prior's House at Hexham Abbey, and he is sometimes referred to as 'of Hexham Abbey'. He probably rented this house from his Wallington relatives, who were the lords of the manor of Hexham.[46] Sir Walter Calverly Blackett had the house much altered and repaired in 1736.

Prior's House, as the name suggests, had been the residence of the Prior of Hexham and was part of the complex of the abbey. Sir Reginald Carnaby had acquired it after the dissolution of the monasteries and converted it into his residence, adding a block of buildings to the west side. By 1600 it belonged to the lord of the manor, Sir John Fenwick. In Sir Edward's time much of the old house built by Prior Leschman, an imposing building with towers, turrets, machicolations and a formidable gateway, remained.

Sir Edward was clearly fond of the house and of Hexham. He had, as we have seen, married the widow of Nicholas Roberts, a merchant. They had no children and appear to have lived quiet lives. He gave £100 to increase the value of the living of Hexham Abbey and filled the interior of the choir with pews and galleries. In 1754 he was granted a licence to convert part of the south transept into a family burial place, and he and his wife were buried there. His stepson, Nicholas Roberts, seems to have lived there until his own death in 1761.

It was, unusually, Sir Edward's younger brother John (1685–1750) who appears to have lived in Newby Hall – a grander hall by far. Appropriately for a third son, he had been set up as a merchant and spent several years in Rotterdam. He became a Hostman and a Merchant Adventurer in Newcastle but, as his entry to both companies was by patrimony, he may well have considered his memberships as honorific. He was known as John Blackett of Newby Hall, but little is known about his time there. In 1748, two years before his death, Newby was sold to the Weddell family. As Sir Edward had no children, it had been clear for some time that John's eldest son would become the fourth baronet on his uncle's death. John and his wife Patience had five sons, and it was the eldest, Edward (1719–1804), who succeeded his uncle in 1756.

The mid-seventeenth century saw a firm shift in the family's centre of gravity from Yorkshire to Northumberland. Newby Hall having been sold to Richard Weddell, the new Sir Edward came to live on his Northumberland estates. These estates had been greatly increased by his marriage to Anne Douglas in 1751.

Anne was the only daughter and the sole heir of Oley Douglas, whose father, John Douglas of Matfen and Newcastle, had bought up the lands of the Carnabys. John Douglas was an attorney in Newcastle and then Town Clerk, in which position he was succeeded by his younger son, Joshua. The position of Town Clerk of Newcastle was a lucrative one or, at least, it provided lucrative opportunities. The Carnabys had acquired Halton Tower in the fourteenth century, and the ruthless Sir Reynold Carnaby had done well out of the dissolution of the monasteries, being Thomas Cromwell's man in the area. He gained land from Hexham Abbey and Brinkburn Priory. A close association with the Earl of Northumberland brought him Percy lands at Langley and Corbridge on favourable long leases. By the late seventeenth century, however, the Carnabys, once so thrusting and hard-headed, were over-extended and their lands heavily mortgaged. Gradually their land was sold off to John Douglas, who bought Halton in 1695, though he allowed John Carnaby to live there until his death five years later. He then bought Aydon Castle in 1702, thus acquiring all the Carnaby lands. Douglas settled these lands upon his son and heir, Oley Douglas, on the occasion of his marriage. Oley Douglas's bride was the daughter of a rich London merchant whom Douglas had met while studying at Gray's Inn. Oley Douglas was MP for Morpeth (1713–15) and contested the Northumberland county election of 1716. He died, however, in 1719, the same year in which his daughter, Anne, was born, when he was only thirty. Her father's early death made Anne Douglas the sole heir, and she, therefore, brought both land and money to her marriage to Edward Blackett, which took place while she was still a ward of Chancery in 1751.[47]

Thus when Sir Edward succeeded his uncle in 1756, he was already a considerable landowner, in possession of several fine houses in Northumberland.[48] From his uncle he inherited Willimoteswick, which, as we have seen, was a small fortified manor house, and Ridley Hall, built as recently as 1743. The Douglas inheritance brought him Aydon Castle, Halton Tower and Matfen Hall. Aydon Castle is essentially a fortified manor house rather than a castle. Perhaps a castle would have been a better idea, for the house was built just as the long period of warfare and disorder along the English–Scottish border began, and defensive capacity was to become crucial. Only a few years after the licence to crenellate was issued in 1305, the hall was taken by the Scots, and not for the last time. Hutchinson

Above Left: Portrait of Mary Yorke, 2nd wife of Sir Edward Blackett, 2nd Bt.

Above: Portrait of John Blackett of Newby, by Michael Dahl.

Above: Portrait of Sir Edward Blackett, 4th Bt. (1719–1804) by Mercier.

Above right: Portrait of Anne Douglas, wife of Sir Edward, by William Hoare of Bath.

described it, a couple of decades after the Blacketts acquired it, as '…now greatly in decay; the situation is formidable, and from the solemnity of its ruins, is at this time strikingly august'.[49] Halton Tower, as it was in Sir Edward's time, still largely consists of a fourteenth-century tower and a late seventeenth-century house attached to the east. There may, however, have been a house at Halton from the Anglo-Saxon period, and what has been referred to as this 'organic house'[50] may well have been inhabited from then. Early and late medieval buildings, and the late seventeenth-century house, were built on top of the Saxon house and one another, adding on to and cannibalizing the masonry of previous houses, as well as using dressed stone from the Roman fort a few hundred yards away.

Above: *The Halton Ox* (1808). This painting of a fine specimen of an improved breed of short-horned cattle was inscribed to Sir William Blackett, Bt., by Thomas Bates, whose lands adjoined Halton and who managed the Halton farms.

It was Matfen Hall, however, which was to be the principal residence of the family for 200 years, although Sir Edward himself didn't spend much time there:

This Sir Edward did not live very much at Matfen, as he bought a villa near Egham [in Surrey] *called Thorpe Lea from Lord Oswell where he and his wife mostly resided; once not coming to the North for a period of six years.*[51]

The West Matfen estate has a long history and in the reigns of King John and Henry III was in the hands of Philip de Ulcote. Hexham Priory also owned land and a church there. The estate passed successively through the hands of the Feltons, the Hastings, the Lawsons and a branch of the Fenwicks[52] before passing to the Douglases. There had been many houses on the site, but the house Sir Edward inherited had been built about 1685 and was described by John Wallis as:

...a neat stone building on a rising ground; a grass slope before it by the riverlet of Pont, crossed by a small bridge; a vista extending from it for two miles to the military road; tall forest trees on each side of the slope for shelter and ornament; a walk of a considerable length to the east with borders of flowers and flowering shrubs.[53]

That contemporary arbiter of taste when it came to country houses and landscapes, William Hutchinson, thought well of Matfen:

Oppsite above: Pen and ink drawing of Aydon Castle, from Lady Alethea's book. She writes: 'It is built on the west side of a deep gill, on the brink of a precipice at whose foot runs a little brook. Aydon was probably built by Peter de Vallibus 1280–1300, though there are remains of a far older castle. It was known as Aydon Hall in the 13th and 14th centuries, and illustrates the domestic architecture of that period, being rather a fortified House than a Castle. The building is surrounded by an outer wall, pierced with arrow holes, and enclosing three courtyards, two larger and one smaller within...'

Oppsite below: Halton Tower, painted in watercolour in Lady Alethea's book.

Above: The Old Matfen House sketched by Sir Edward Blackett, 6th Bt.

Right: Old Matfen, from Lady Alethea's book.

... the estate of Sir Edward Blackett, whose mansion-house is seated on a fine eminence, shielded by extensive woods, above the river Pont, with a vista of considerable extent opening upon the military road. The house and pleasure grounds are highly pleasing, though not pompous; there is that elegance which perfect neatness constitutes to be discerned in the whole.[54]

The careers of Sir Edward's brothers demonstrate the degree to which the Blacketts had settled into the conventional pattern of a gentry family. The second brother, William, became an army officer, serving with the 22nd regiment of foot; the third, Henry, went to Oxford University and then became Rector of Boldon; while the youngest brother, John Erasmus, returned to the family's roots and became a prominent Newcastle merchant. Matthew also became a merchant, but was drowned at sea.

It is John Erasmus who is best remembered and whose name is commemorated in Newcastle's Blackett Street, built some twenty years after his death. He seems to have been apprenticed to a Liverpool merchant and then become a partner of Alderman Simson, a leading coal dealer in Newcastle. Prominent in public life, he was, towards the end of the Seven Years War, a captain and the paymaster of the Northumberland Militia, and he became an Alderman and a Mayor of Newcastle. He married Sarah, the daughter of William Roddam of Hethpool. The Roddams were one of the oldest families in Northumberland and were already landowners at the time of the Conquest. He was on good terms with Sir Walter Calverly Blackett, who gave him stewardship of his lead mines, a post of considerable profit.

Above: Portrait of Sarah Roddam, by Allan Ramsay.

Right: Portrait of John Erasmus Blackett, by David Martin.

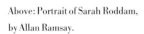

We have a description of John Erasmus, but it comes from the jaundiced eye of his brother-in-law, the Reverend Dr Alexander Carlyle, Minister of Inveresk, who found fault with most people unless they were great aristocrats or part of the select circle of Edinburgh *literati*. As we have seen, he had characterized Sir Walter Calverly Blackett as 'not a man of remarkable parts' and he found John Erasmus 'imperfectly educated…and of ordinary talents',[55] but he approved of his brother Henry, 'a good scholar and a very agreeable man of the world'. Carlyle obviously found Newcastle society somewhat rough and ready, the men 'ill educated while the ladies, who were bred in the south, by their appearance and manners, seemed to be very unequally yoked'.[56]

John Erasmus's daughter, Sarah, married Cuthbert Collingwood, later Vice-Admiral Lord Collingwood. The story is told that when Collingwood was a mere lieutenant and she plain Mrs Collingwood, Sarah was presented at Court, and someone made to introduce her to Mrs Beaumont, whose husband, Colonel Beaumont, had by then inherited the Blackett lead mines. The haughty Diana snubbed her, making a dismissive remark to the effect that this was just her steward's daughter. When some years later Mrs, now Lady, Collingwood, was again at Court, Mrs Beaumont came up to her and was snubbed in her turn. It was an expensive gesture, for Mrs Beaumont rushed back to Northumberland and sacked John Erasmus Blackett from his lucrative position.[56]

Always fashionably dressed and fond of good living, John Erasmus Blackett spent his money freely and could never resist a business speculation. Lord Collingwood became somewhat exasperated with his father-in-law when he found out that

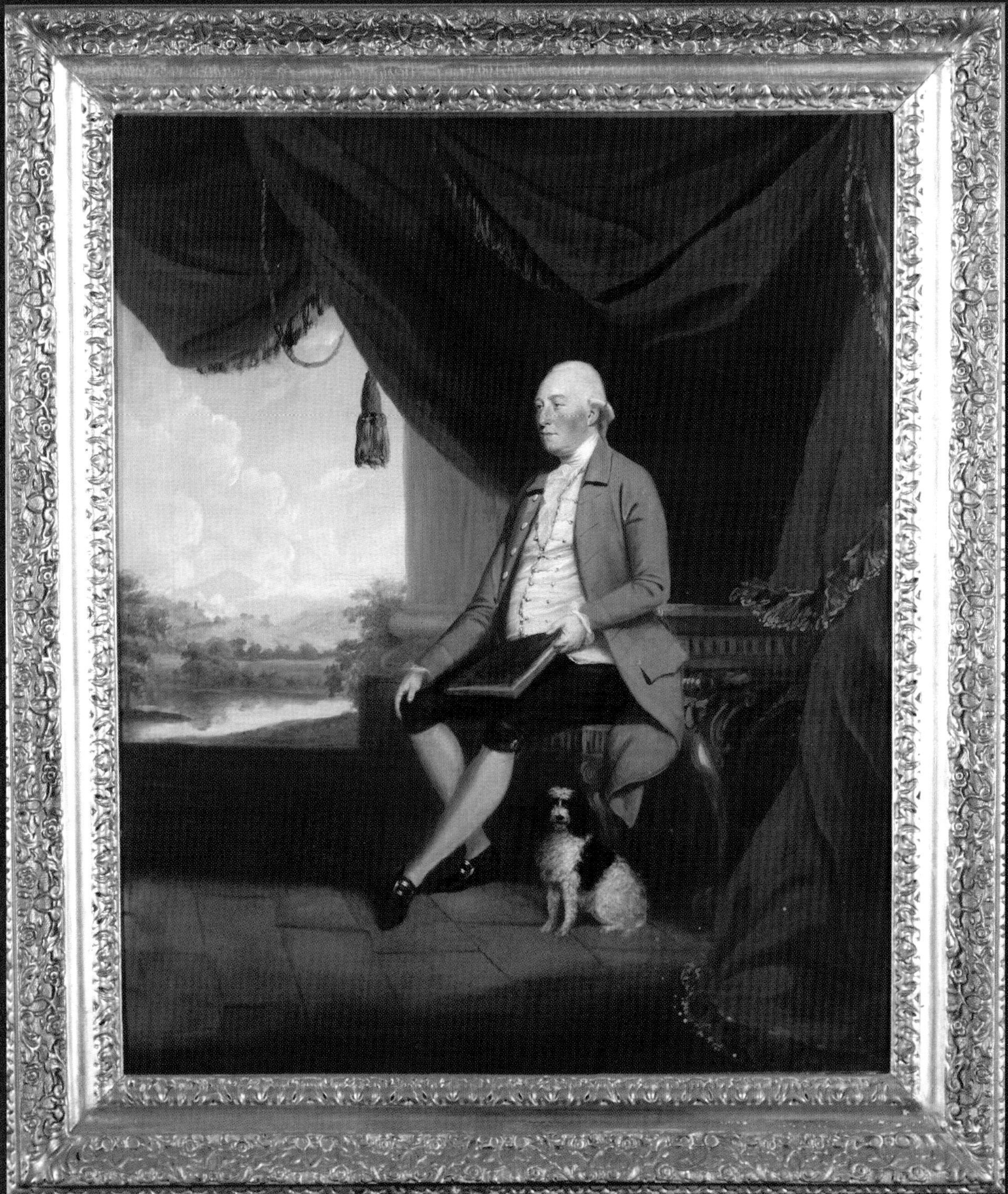

Blackett had pledged his credit to the tune of £2200, and he also felt that he had passed on his extravagant habits to his daughter: 'My wife would gladly confine herself to what I prescribe, but the gaiety, the vanity and the love of feeding of her father, there is no bounds to'.[58] The admiral, however, got on very well with Sir Edward, who became one of his favourite correspondents, and he often stayed with him.

With their enlarged estate and their new seat at Matfen Hall, the line descended from Sir Edward Blackett, 2nd Bt., though not quite as grand as that headed by Sir Walter Blackett, which was descended from Sir Edward's younger brother, Sir William, was among the first rank of the Northumberland gentry. Great wealth usually results in an investment in education and culture, and in the eighteenth century it became almost essential for rich young men to acquire the polish that could come only from travel, and in particular from time spent in Italy. Edward, the oldest child of Sir Edward Blackett, 4th Bt., lived abroad for much of his life, while William, who eventually succeeded to the baronetcy, made the Grand Tour. He brought back several works of art from Rome that adorned Matfen Hall.

William's twin sister, Anne, eloped with Major (later General) William Scott, the greatgrandson of Sir Edward Blackett, 2nd Bt., but her father seems to have accepted the match and bought the couple Thorpe House, close to the Blacketts' Surrey residence, Thorpe Lea. This marriage was to add to the Blackett blood in Alethea Blackett, the family historian, who was the granddaughter of Anne.

Though he spent much of the time in Surrey, Sir Edward, 4th Bt. was interested in Matfen and determined to improve it. In a letter to his young grandchild, Patience Scott, the elderly baronet describes the work that was taking place to widen the

River Pont, which ran in front of the house '…making several cascades in it, to heighten the water, that it may all be seen from the house'.[59] Major Scott, the young Patience's father, seems to have been left in charge of the Matfen estate while Sir Edward was away, and was responsible for these alterations to the river; he had already seen to a major change, the move of the main entrance from the south to the west.[60]

William, who had married Mary-Anne Keane in 1801, inherited the Blackett estates along with the baronetcy in 1804. Like the previous generation, Sir William and his wife seem to have lived mainly at Thorpe Lea, but Sir William died in 1816 when his heir, Edward, was only eleven, and Mary-Anne, a most capable and intelligent woman, managed the family's affairs until Edward's majority. She devoted much attention to improving the Matfen estate. Matfen Hall was already surrounded by fine trees, many of them planted by Sir Edward, 4th Bt., but letters from John Ridley, steward for the estate, refer to the creation of a new plantation beside the Standing Stone, an upright stone pillar some three-quarters of a mile from the house amid a circular mound, and to the diversion of the road to give the house greater privacy:

Honoured Lady – I have delayed writing upon the event of the road being diverted that leads past Matfen Hall- which will be determined tomorrow – On account of so much business at Court, the road did not come on till Friday when I have the

Above: Portrait of Mary-Anne Ruck Keane, wife of Sir William Blackett.
Artist unknown.

Below: Portrait of Sir William Blackett, 5th Bt. (*d.*1816)

happiness to announce to your ladyship it passed the court and of course we will proceed to plant and make the new road as soon as the weather will permit.[61]

Sir William died in 1816 and was succeeded by his second son, Edward. He was to enjoy his inheritance for a long time. By the mid-1820s he was serving as an officer in that most fashionable of regiments, the Life Guards. This was pleasant in peacetime, especially for a man with a large income, and, being based near Windsor, Edward was able to join fully in the stylish society life of London, where he had a house in Portman Street. His diary for June 1828 attests to his attendance at parties given by Lady Burgoyne, the Duke of Northumberland, Lady Sheffield and the heir to the throne, the Duke of Clarence. He had ample leave, which enabled him to spend time in Northumberland, and, if he was not able to attend every meet of the Northumberland Fox-hounds, the dates of which were neatly entered in his diaries, he was able to record early in 1830 that he had hunted with them thirteen times during the season.[62] Clearly a fit man and a keen sportsman, he records skating on ponds at Matfen and Belsay, and participation in cricket matches whenever the opportunity offered. If he was at home in London society, he was also on good terms with his Northumberland neighbours, the Allgoods at Nunwick, the Blacketts of Wylam, the Trevelyans of Netherwitton and Sir Charles Monck of Belsay, whose daughter he was to marry.

As we have seen, Edward's father, Sir William, had gone on the Grand Tour, an enterprise that was considered to provide an almost essential finish to a gentleman's

Portrait of Sir Edward Blackett, 6th Bt. (1805–1885), in Life Guards' uniform, by Hurlstone.

Portrait of Julia Monck, by Janet Ross.

Watercolour of Belsay, from Arthur Edward Blackett's game book.

education. The great age of the Grand Tour was undoubtedly the eighteenth century, and potential tourists had found themselves unable to visit the continent after the early 1790s because of the French Revolutionary and Napoleonic Wars. Edward's friend and future father-in-law, Sir Charles Monck, had, however, been adventurous enough to honeymoon in Greece in 1804–6 and had built Belsay Hall in the style of a Greek temple. After the peace of 1815 tourists once more flocked to France, Switzerland, Germany and Italy, and in the summer of 1830, Sir Edward, with his bride, Julia Monck, embarked on the mail packet at Dover for a honeymoon that would last more than a year. This tour took the couple along the well-trodden route that had been established as obligatory for well-educated and well-connected tourists. They attended courts, went to the balls and receptions of both local notabilities and expatriates, visited the ruins of past glories and appreciated sunsets on Swiss lakes. Sir Edward went to see the battlefield of Waterloo, where Wellington had triumphed fifteen years earlier, played cricket at Geneva, admired Pompeii and bought *objets d'art*. In Naples, almost a British colony, the couple attended the tableaux at Lady Acton's and the theatricals at Lady Drummond's, and met up with Julia's father, for Sir Charles Monck was visiting Naples and Sicily at the same time. The return to England reveals a tough traveller, who, on arrival in London, after a passage across the channel and a coach from Dover, was still able to attend Lady Ridley's ball.

Even before his marriage Sir Edward had been preoccupied by architectural ambitions. Among his many estates was land to the north of the Roman Wall, at the western

extremity of the Middle March and close to Bewcastle Waste. Here, beside the wild beauty of Greenlee Lough and the grimly named Gallowshield Rigg, Sir Edward had decided to build a shooting lodge. He had already employed John Dobson, the leading architect in the north east, to make alterations to the Dower House at Matfen, and his diary entry for New Year's Day 1829 reads 'went to Gallowshield Rigg with Mr Dobson and fixed upon a situation for a shooting box'. Some shooting box! Bonny Rigg Hall was to be an imposing house with a drawing room, a dining room, a business room or study, eight bedrooms for family and guests, extensive servants' quarters, which included a butler's pantry and a servants' hall, and a coach house and stables.

Rather more important to Sir Edward were his plans for his principal residence. A mania for building has been a characteristic of the British aristocracy and gentry, and perhaps of the rich and powerful in every country and culture. Houses and estates were a projection of oneself, and of one's wealth, status and taste. If this urge led to overspending and even bankruptcies, contemporaries had reason to be grateful for the employment it created, as has posterity for the legacy of so many fine houses and landscapes. It says much for the prosperity of Northumberland agriculture that Sir Edward was able to spend £70,000 on rebuilding Matfen Hall.

English agriculture was enormously prosperous in the second half of the eighteenth century and during the Napoleonic Wars, but suffered a long post-war decline, only to achieve prosperity again in the high-farming period of the mid-nineteenth century. Northumberland survived the post-war decline better than most counties, and added to its reputation as a centre for progressive farming with the innovative methods introduced by John Grey of Dilston, and the success of

102 Bonny Rigg, *c.*1910.

Thomas Bates in breeding spectacularly large shorthorn cattle. Bates, who lived and farmed at Aydon White House, also looked after the Blacketts' farms at Halton during Sir Edward's minority.

Sir Edward, who began the rebuilding of his mansion in 1832, was more than its commissioner or even its patron, for he was a knowledgeable architect himself. In this he resembled his father-in-law, who had been his own architect at Belsay Hall. It may seem surprising that, instead of commissioning John Dobson, the most fashionable architect in the north, and the man with whom he had entrusted Bonny Rigg, he should instead have chosen the Birmingham architect Thomas Rickman. Just about everyone who was having a country house built in Northumberland was employing Dobson, who was happy to design in a variety of styles. He was the architect of such varied houses as Doxford Hall (1818) and Mitford Hall (1823), with their Doric columns; Longhirst Hall (1824), with its Corinthian portico and pediment; Tudor-style Cheeseburn Grange (1813); and Tudor-Gothic Lilburn Tower (1828–29). Sir Edward had almost certainly intended to employ Dobson as the architect for Matfen, but he had good reason to be dissatisfied with Dobson's work on Bonny Rigg. The house looked well enough but the roof leaked – so badly that it had to be replaced. No doubt Dobson was very busy when Bonny Rigg was being built, for work on St Thomas's Church (1827–30) in Newcastle and on Lilburn Tower in north Northumberland would still have been going on. In addition there must have been special problems with the building of Bonny Rigg, which was out in the wilds and difficult for experienced builders, joiners and, indeed, roofers to get to. Nevertheless, the fact that the house had a defective roof made Sir Edward

Design for Bonny Rigg by John Dobson, 1829.

disinclined to employ Dobson again. At dinner with a bishop, Sir Edward raised the problem of finding an architect for Matfen, and the bishop suggested he might think of Thomas Rickman, whose work as an ecclesiastical architect the bishop admired. The suggestion was acted upon.

Thomas Rickman was an historian as well as an architect, and had published *An Attempt to Discriminate the Styles of English Architecture* (1817). His admiration for Early English details seems, according to the leading experts on John Dobson, to have influenced Dobson when he designed St Thomas's, and the two architects had similar interests:

Like Dobson and many other architects of the time, Rickman seems to have had an equal liking for both the Greek and the Gothic styles but wished especially to facilitate modern Gothic church design. He divided English medieval architecture into four main phases – 'Norman', 'Early English', 'Decorated', and 'Perpendicular' – thus providing the terminology still in use today.[63]

The relationship between Rickman and the man who commissioned him was not, however, to be a happy one. Probably Sir Edward knew too much about architecture not to interfere, and, later, successfully designed the church at Matfen himself. As Alethea Blackett recounted:

Sir Edward began by employing Mr Rickman of Birmingham, architect, but having disagreed with him on his wishing to pull down the old house before commencing the new one, and also differing on the general designs of the house, Sir Edward dismissed him, took the matter into his own hands, and the house was finally built from Sir Edward's own designs.

Rickman wished for Gothic, Sir Edward determined upon Elizabethan with a Gothic Hall. He continued to superintend every detail of the building. The house took four years to build.

Robinson of Pooley Bridge was the builder. The masons were partly Scotch, partly English.

The best stone was quarried from Black Pasture, Brunton Bank, a sandstone.[64]

Alethea may have somewhat exaggerated Sir Edward's role, for the greater part of the house was to Rickman's design, although the owner certainly continued the work after his quarrel with his architect.

The completed house was large and imposing with its gables and its mullioned and transomed windows. Essentially it is an eclectic historicist fantasy; a statement in stone, not just of early nineteenth-century wealth and authority, but of taste; and

Matfen Hall completed.

an interpretation of history. Matfen dominates the surrounding countryside. The two-mile-long road from Matfen Piers to the Hall and village is bordered with trees and acts as a *vallée d'honneur*, leading to the carefully landscaped park and across the Pont to the ornate gates of the park. A heavy, carved doorway, surmounted by the Blackett coat of arms, provides entrance to the Gothic Hall, while in turn the echoing mock-medieval grandeur of the hall gives way to the comforts of the dining room, library and drawing rooms, with the south-facing windows overlooking the terrace and the River Pont.

The entrance is on the North side. You enter into a small hall, which opens into the great one, the height of which is 56 feet – it has an open oaken Gothic roof – an open upper arcaded gallery runs round two sides of the Hall, supported on one side by stone pillars and pointed arches of Edward III Gothic, on the other side is the fire place. The staircase occupies the two remaining sides. [65]

From its first furnishing the house had a museum-like quality. As Alethea Blackett put it, 'the hall was fitted up with armour from various periods'. She has left us a thorough inventory: family portraits, souvenirs from Sir William's Grand Tour, relics from the real and mythical history of the north east, and purchases by the new Sir Edward at London sales: a sword of the Carnabys and the sword or falchion with which Sir John Conyers of Sockburn, County Durham, is supposed to have slain the wyverne, or dragon; a more modern weapon, a fearsome and deadly double-headed piece of shot fired from a Spanish ship on to Collingwood's ship at Trafalgar; a Florentine

Left: 'You enter into a small hall, which opens onto the great one…'

Right: Matfen's Gothic Hall, as shown in a drawing in pen and ink from Lady Alethea's book.

shield bought at Christies; a Caravaggio, a Van Dyck and a Rubens; and a white marble fireplace by Chantrey, originally ordered for Buckingham Palace.

Sir Edward, having built his house, based himself firmly in Northumberland, although he retained a London town house, moving from Portman Street to the even grander Portman Square. The town houses in Portman Square were palatial and among them were those built for the Countess of Home and Mrs Montagu. Number 34, Sir Edward's house, had been built for the Duke of Gloucester. Edward's younger brother John Charles, a naval officer, took over at Thorpe Lea, which was eventually sold on his death in 1896. Another brother, Henry Collingwood, took over Sockburn, where his mother, the widowed Lady Blackett, had a house built for him in 1833.

There is an irony in the fact that the Blacketts made much of the Sockburn connection, with its antiquity and legends, while being cavalier with the place itself. Writing in 1941 and recalling Wordsworth's sojourn at Sockburn before he established himself in the Lake District, Una Pope-Henessy imagined how indignant the poet would have been at the 'big stone mansion in Abbotsford Gothic' built a few decades later, and castigates Henry Collingwood Blackett:

The builder of the Hall had the temerity to remove from the chapel to the house 'the statue of the armed knight', and he also reduced the church to the diminished ruin it is today.[66]

Left: The Gothic Hall at Matfen. *Photograph from Lady Alethea's book.*

Far left: Sockburn Hall, c.1910.

Bottom left: Matfen Church. *Photograph from Lady Alethea's book.*

Right: The Sockburn Falchion. *Photograph by kind permission of Durham Cathedral Chapter.*

Tastes in architecture change and Una Pope-Henessy was writing before the revived appreciation of nineteenth-century architecture. It is by no means certain, either, that Wordsworth, a friend of Sir Walter Scott, would have disapproved of 'Abbotsford Gothic'. Henry Collingwood Blackett was, however, certainly philistine in his treatment of the attractive and historic pink sandstone church that stood close by. As Alethea Blackett, who like Sir Edward, delighted in the family's association with Sockburn, with its history and legend, relates:

After the house was built Mr Blackett disliked the little church being so near and procured the leave of the Bishop to pull it down on condition that he built another which he did an ugly poor little building on the top of a hill on the other side of the river.[67]

Sockburn later became the home of Sir Edward Blackett's grandson, Arthur Blackett, and remained in the possession of the family until the mid-twentieth century.

Sir Edward took on the normal duties of a Northumberland landowner, becoming a Deputy Lord Lieutenant of the county and a JP, and participated fully in the social life of the county. By his first wife, Julia, he had two sons and five daughters. Her early death at the age of thirty-three must have been a great blow. His second marriage was again within the Northumberland gentry. Frances Vere was the daughter of Sir William Lorraine of Kirkharle and the widow of William Henry

THE BLACKETTS OF NEWBY HALL AND MATFEN

Ord MP of Whitfield. Edward married her in 1851. 'Fanny' was five years older than Sir Edward. There was no Grand Tour honeymoon after their marriage but rather quiet days spent walking around Bonny Rigg, which set the tone for this companionable marriage that ended with Fanny's death in 1874. The third marriage, to Isabella Helen, daughter of John Richardson of Kirklands, Roxburghshire, lasted only four years until Isabella's death in 1879.

Above: Matfen church and village in the 1890s.

Far Left: Matfen Hall today.

It was not just the house that was subject to Sir Edward's architectural interests. He also reconstructed the village and designed its Holy Trinity Church. The village became very much an estate village, constructed on an idealized model of how a village should look, with its Tudor-style cottages overlooking the green and stream. The result has been criticized as alien to Northumberland: 'Thus Matfen became a traditional village of the midlands and the south with the church and big house in close association'.[68] The church was built in Early English style, and the first edition of Pevsner's *The Buildings of England* suggested that the spire 'would look in place somewhere in the Nene valley'. The latest edition, however, describes the church as 'quite powerful with its very high broach spire'.[69] Purists for the vernacular may criticize Sir Edward's efforts at Matfen, but most of his contemporaries found it charming, as do modern visitors:

This charming little village, from its sheltered position and sweet rural attractions, bids fair to become a favourite resort of the dwellers of our large towns in need of rest and quiet. It is agreeably remote from the sound of the railway whistle, and still retains some of the old Arcadian peace and simplicity.[70]

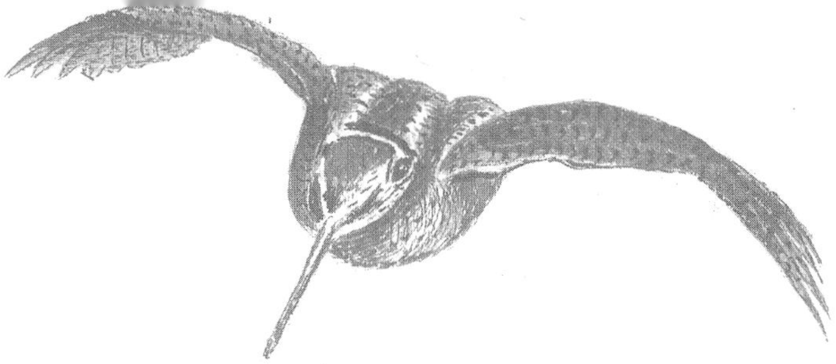

This 'Arcadian peace' was far from constant, as for many years there was a large number of Irish navvies in the area working on the complex and ambitious schemes of the Newcastle and Gateshead Water Company, to bring water via tunnels from Ryal and Whittington to Whittle Dene Reservoir. The Black Bull Inn was kept busy at all hours and there were some spectacular disturbances. One fight in the pub was ended only when a villager inserted a swarm of bees through a window. The water companies did, however, provide the final touch to the village's picturesque quality in the shape of the man-made stream that runs through it.

Sir Edward's improvements at Matfen were an expression of a social vision, shared by many of his contemporary landowners, of a harmonious, if layered, society, where the big house and church presided over prosperous farmers and a contented agricultural workforce. This strong vein of paternalism resulted in a considerable improvement in rural housing in Northumberland, as the very basic, heather-thatched cottages, common early in the nineteenth century, gave way to model villages with roomier and solidly built houses with gardens, and with common social facilities, including reading rooms – as at Matfen – and village halls.

Aged seventy-four at the time of the death of his third wife in February 1879, Sir Edward was still vigorous enough to contemplate a fourth marriage, and his choice was a young woman whom he must have known for most of her life, Alethea Scott. The Scotts were, as we have seen, related to the Blacketts and lived close to the Blacketts' Surrey home of Thorpe Lea. Sir Edward and Alethea were married in August 1880.

Not everyone was delighted at the match, and Mary Elizabeth Lucy wrote of it in vinegar, though she admired Sir Edward's town house:

The next evening I was to dine in Portman Square with Sir Edward and Lady Blackett to meet my brother William and his wife. … When the door bell was rung two tall fine powdered footmen appeared and ushered me into a splendid drawing room, the walls hung with the most beautiful tapestry I ever saw in this country. The colours were just as fresh as though it had been just done, whereas it was more than a hundred years old, the possessor having been the Duke of Gloucester, brother of George III, for whom the house had been purchased, and decorated by Italian artists. Some of the panels were painted exquisitely, as well as the ceiling.

Lady Blackett is 40 years younger than Sir Edward, who has had three if not four wives, and the curious thing is that when she first came out she was engaged to Sir Edward Blackett's eldest son who jilted her. She is sister to my brother Willy's wife. Sir Edward is a regular made-up old dandy, with a wig, false teeth and very crotchety on his legs! But what does that matter? When a man, however old, has a fine house in the country, ditto in London and a fine income, he can always get a wife, and I am sorry to say a young one too if he wishes it. A rich old woman also can get a penniless young man for her husband, for instance the poor Baroness Cheque Book, as an American named the Baroness Burdett Coutts.[71]

Mrs Lucy, who was only two years younger than Sir Edward and feeling her age, was, no doubt, a far from impartial observer. Marriages between elderly men and young women were far from rare, but the gossip about Alethea having been jilted by her husband's son must have been widespread.

The previous engagement to Edward William Blackett made Alethea's position in

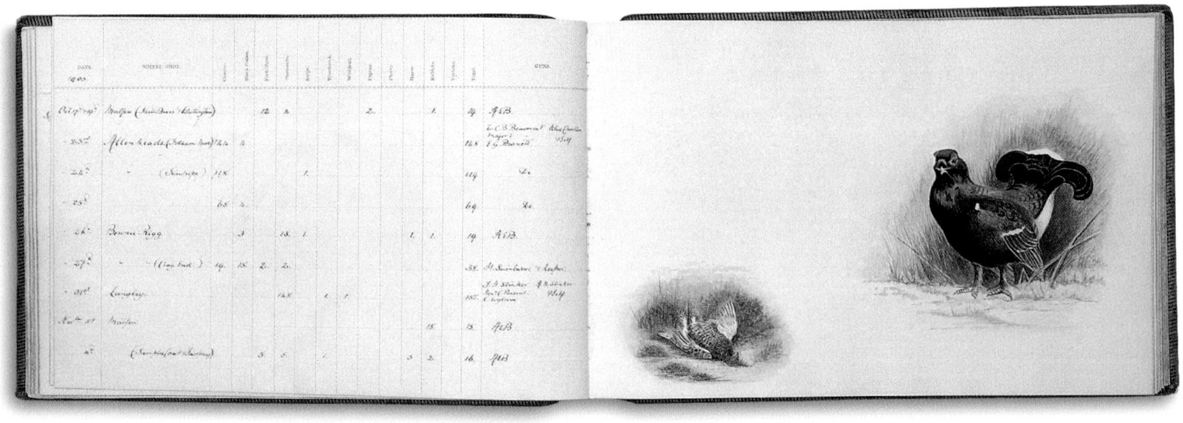

114 Pages from the 'Game book' of A. Blackett with an illustration of a black cock.

the Blackett family somewhat unusual.[72] The son and heir had, by the time of Alethea's marriage, produced four children by his wife, Julia, a daughter of Lord Somerville. This must have added to the family tensions that were not uncommon when elderly gentlemen with grown-up children and grandchildren remarried. Edward William was, however, away from Matfen most of the time as he was engaged in a successful and distinguished career.

After an education at Eton he had been gazetted to an ensigncy in the 13th Light Infantry, and having been promoted to lieutenant, sailed with the Rifle Brigade for the Crimea in 1855. He saw plenty of bloody fighting in the abysmal conditions that the British army had to endure before Sebastopol, and was present in all the main engagements, Alma, Balaclava and Inkerman. Eventually, he was seriously wounded while leading a ladder party in the desperate attack on the Russian stronghold, the Redan Fort. He was invalided home but his left leg had to be amputated. He did not allow his disability to stand in the way of a successful military career. He went on to become a captain in 1855, a major in 1862, a lieutenant colonel, a colonel in 1878 and a major-general in 1889. If his early steps up the ladder would have been by purchase, as was the system of the day, he was clearly an outstanding officer whose merit and valour were recognized in the high rank he achieved. He was forty when he married, but did not retire from the army until several years after his father's death.

The marriage between Alethea and her elderly husband appears to have been successful enough, if brief. Alethea was nearing forty when she married and was not really the young girl portrayed by Mrs Lucy. Her marital chances must have faded, and

Left: Photograph of Major-General Sir Edward William Blackett, 7th Bt.

Below: Photograph of Julia Somerville (m. 1871, d. 1913), his wife.

the opportunity to become mistress of Matfen and to be left well-provided for with title and station after her husband's death must have been attractive. She must have known her husband well, having been brought up at Thorpe House, close to Thorpe Lea at which Sir Edward was a frequent visitor. It is clear that she revelled in her new position and was entranced by life at Matfen and by the houses and possessions of her husband.

During her short reign at Matfen she witnessed the Indian summer of the great country house. Although the agricultural depression, which began in the 1870s, has been seen retrospectively as marking the beginning of the end for great landowners, houses continued to be kept and run in grand style. In Northumberland, where much of the land was suited to pastoral farming, rents did not fall so catastrophically as in corn-producing counties. If anything, big houses in Northumberland became bigger with the addition of new wings and ballrooms. There were plenty of servants to run them and with central heating systems fuelled by cheap coal they were easily made comfortable.

Matfen, like other big houses, was the centre of a whole world and a local economy that stretched for miles around, connecting the farms and hamlets to the house. The inner circle was formed by the household staff, indoor and outdoor, which formed a society of its own with an elaborate hierarchy and system of codes. For most male and some female servants, service was a career, and butlers and housekeepers were powerful figures. For many female servants service was a stage in life, a spell between childhood and marriage.

Provided all seemed to run smoothly, the wise master or mistress did not interfere too much with what went on behind the green baize door, though those who ignored the servants' world altogether could find themselves with ill-run or disorderly houses. A good butler and/or housekeeper was essential, but these were not always easy to find. Even the best of butlers had a tendency to take to drink and, even if not inebriates,

Below left: The garden walkway.

Right: The Dutch Garden.

Far right: The garden front at Matfen, *c.* 1880, from Lady Alethea's book.

to divert the better wines in the cellar to their own use. Then there were the sexual mores of a household. At one Northumberland house the mistress was mortified to learn that for many years the laundry had been operating as a brothel. The novelist Catherine Cookson based much of her literary success upon the theme of the seduction of the female servant by the young master, but sexual relationships between servants were far more common.[73]

A further problem with servants was privacy; the green baize door and the 'dumb waiter' were invented to preserve a family's privacy, but they afforded little protection, and everyone in a neighbourhood knew the secrets of the big house. The families of such houses were a constant subject of local gossip. In a sense they were like mini-royal families and had their popular and unpopular members,

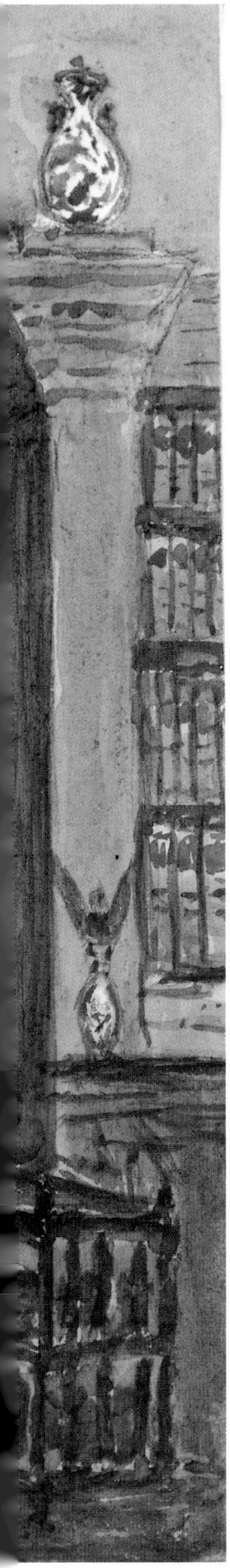

Painting in watercolour and gouache of the library chimneypiece, with a lady seated beside the fire, from Lady Alethea's book. She writes: 'The chimney piece carved back in the time of Queen Elizabeth, is supported by caryatids, representing Bacchus and Ceres, was bought at Well and Craig, Old Bond Street. It must have belonged to the house of the Lees of Woodstock, as the arms of the family are carved in one of the panels. Among the various objects that hang between the chimney piece and book cases are two brass bas reliefs, Dutch subjects bought at Moses in Oxford Street; and two bronze bas reliefs bought in a marine store shop at Milan. The bronze pheasant was bought in the French department of the International Exhibition in London 1851. These with the other objects were bought by Sir Edward.'

depending on to whom one listened: Mr So-and-So was a 'right lad', one young lady was 'ever so sweet and thoughtful', while another was 'arrogant and demanding'; one daughter of the house was shortly to be engaged to a neighbouring landowner but another's expectations of a proposal had been disappointed; or the master of the house had had a terrible row with his son over the latter's gambling debts. Servants were, however, essential and Alethea, used to servants but to much smaller numbers of them, would have had to learn how to preside over the dozens at Matfen and Portman Square.

Sir Edward was fond of London life during the season, so the year alternated between time spent at Matfen and a lengthy sojourn at Portman Square. In addition there were visits to other houses and it was usual to entertain large numbers of visitors. House parties often centred on shooting and Sir Edward was a keen sportsman. There was shooting and fishing at Matfen itself but Sir Edward was fond of his shooting lodge at Bonny Rigg Hall,[74] which provided not only splendid opportunities for shooting but also for fishing in Greenlee

The library at Matfen, *c.* 1880, from Lady Alethea's book.

Top left and right: The library at Matfen in the 1890s.

Bottom left: The drawing room, with the fireplace by Chantry originally intended for Buckingham Palace.

Bottom right: The dining room.

Opposite: 34 Portman Square, c. 1910.
Photograph courtesy of City of Westminster Archives.

and the other loughs close by. Shooting was, even more than hunting, an inseparable part of the aristocratic and gentry life style. The *grande battue* had come to dominate shooting, and Sir Edward, who kept a detailed account of his bags in his game book, demanded plenty of birds when he entertained guests. It was the job of his many gamekeepers to provide the right amount of sport.[75] Nevertheless, he went out shooting most days in most weeks in the season and seems to have been just as happy to go out with a gun, his dogs and a companion or two on his or neighbours' estates. Bags of hundreds of birds and hares alternate in his game book with those of a dozen or so partridges and a few hares.

As we have seen, Alethea delighted in the history of the Blackett family, but she was also fascinated by the many houses the Blacketts of Matfen owned and by the beauties of the as yet unspoiled countryside of west Northumberland. Hoppyland and Newby Hall were long gone and Sockburn had passed to a cadet branch of the family, but Sir Edward Blackett still owned – as well as Matfen Hall and a dower house at Matfen – Halton Tower, Aydon Castle, Willimoteswick, the house in Portman Square and the shooting

lodge Bonny Rigg Hall. With the images from brush and camera captured in her book, she has left us a record of this great estate: the manicured lawns, the decorative and productive gardens of Matfen; the jewel of discreet Halton; Aydon, then a farmhouse, still romantic in its setting and the resonance of siege and battle; sturdy Willimoteswick; and the rugged beauty of Bonny Rigg overlooking Greenlee Lough and the Roman Wall.

Above: Watercolour of Greenlee Lough from Lady Alethea's book.

Next page
Top left: Aydon Castle, *c.* 1880.

Top right: Halton Tower, *c.* 1880.

Right: Beltingham, *c.* 1880. Willimoteswick is close to Beltingham village.

A key to understanding Alethea's love for the Blackett estates and houses is that she had come to know them many years before her marriage. As we have seen, Anne, the daughter of Sir Edward Blackett, 4th Bt., had married General William Scott of Thorpe House, Surrey. Their son, William Henry Scott, who also became a general, married Harriot Alethea, daughter of the first Lord Stanley of Alderley, and Alethea was their second daughter. General William Henry Scott and Sir Edward Blackett were, therefore, cousins and the families had remained quite close, seeing each other at Egham, while the Scotts visited Sir Edward in Northumberland.

In the early 1860s, Alethea's mother, Harriot Alethea, seems to have preferred to spend the late summers abroad, leaving her husband to proceed to the north of England and Scotland with his grown-up son and daughters for holidays that combined shooting and sight-seeing. On at least two occasions, they stayed with Sir Edward and his second wife, Frances Vere. General Scott, in affectionate and amusing letters to his wife, described their stays at Matfen and Bonny Rigg. Matfen Hall he thought was very fine, but he related that the 'young ladies', as he referred to his daughters, were not kind to the new house and thought Halton Castle or Aydon Castle would have been better places to build the principal house. He describes a drive to Aydon:

You pass along the Roman road about four or five miles, then come to a large Roman Encampment – then to Halton Castle, a mere square tower but beautifully situated – which was the place for the house the Girls say. Aydon Castle a mile further on is romantically placed; on two sides a precipitate ravine full of trees, a small brook running in the bottom – we had numerous perils to get on the Battlements, passed through a small aperture, where no crinoline had passed before, and were well recompensed...[76]

Another year found General Scott and his daughters, Marian and Alethea (his son William and his younger daughter, Adela, were with their mother in France), at Bonny Rigg; 'Here we are very happy, and in a very nice place'. The father fished in the lough and shot grouse with Sir Edward and his other guests, though the shooting was poor that year, while his daughters went riding 'with their new cousins who appear very fond of them'. Their departure for Scotland was put off for a few days

Bonny Rigg, from Lady Alethea's book.

Borcovicus on the Wall, from Lady Alethea's book.

'because the cousins have become such friends that there would have been great distress'. There were many excursions: a walk with the Keeper to Borcovicus, 'formerly a Roman station on the wall; it is the property of Mr Clayton, a very rich man'; and a ride to Willimoteswick, which involved crossing the Tyne at a shallow point. The mile-long Greenlee Lough was good for boating as well as fishing, and Alethea 'showed off' her prowess and 'rowed a party of visitors to the top and back again'.[77]

Happy recollections from visits to Northumberland with her much-loved father, when she was in her early twenties, thus formed a backdrop to Alethea's time as the wife of the elderly Sir Edward. Bonny Rigg seems to have had a special attraction

Sir Hugh Blackett, 8th Bt. (1873–1960).

for her. This is not surprising given the wild and glorious scenery around the house, but perhaps it was there that she encountered Edward William and began the relationship that would end with a broken engagement. It was, in any case, to her in the early 1880s, a place full of memories as well as present satisfactions.

Sir Edward died in 1885 and Alethea's time as mistress of Matfen was over. She married again three years later. Her new husband, Henry Gisborne Holt of Ropeley Grove, Hampshire, was a little younger than she. She continued to maintain her identity as Alethea, Lady Blackett, as well as Mrs Holt, and continued her research into the history of the Blacketts until her death in 1920.

Right: Photograph of Major-General Sir Edward William Blackett, his wife, Julia, and their son, Sir Hugh Douglas, sitting outside at Matfen, *c.*1890.

Top right: Julia Blackett, wife of Sir E W Blackett, in the garden at Matfen, *c.*1890.

The grand style of the Blacketts of Matfen was to be maintained long after Sir Edward's death by his son, Major-General Sir Edward William Blackett, and his grandson Sir Hugh Douglas, who died in 1960. But perhaps Alethea had seen the high tide of the Northumberland gentry.

Left: Major-General Sir E.W. Blackett.

Bottom left: Major-General Sir E.W Blackett in an open carriage outside Matfen, *c.*1890.

Below: Charles Douglas, the eldest son of Sir Hugh Blackett, on a Shetland pony, *c.*1910.

3. THE BLACKETTS OF WYLAM

As chance would have it, the line of the eldest brother of the first Sir William Blackett, Christopher Blackett, and the heirs of Sir William became near neighbours in the Tyne Valley. In the mid-eighteenth century a great swathe of the land between Newburn and Haltwhistle must have belonged to the Blacketts. As the eldest son, Christopher inherited the family estates and he also followed that pathway to wealth and property, advantageous marriage. His wife, Alice, was the sole heir to Thomas Fenwick of East Matfen, and, on his father-in-law's death, Christopher inherited the manor of Wylam.

Christopher himself cannot have enjoyed this legacy for long, as he died in 1675, and it does not appear as though his eldest son, William, enjoyed this inheritance

128 The river wall at Wylam Scars, drawn by J.W. Carmichael. From *Views of Newcastle and Carlisle Railway* (1836).

Above right: Wylam Hall in 1873.
Photograph courtesy of Philip Brooks.

Far right: Wylam Old Colliery in 1868.
Photograph courtesy of Philip Brooks.

either. William had an adventurous career. He was indentured as an apprentice Merchant Adventurer in 1649, and his first master was his uncle Edward Blackett, but on account of Edward's long residence in Amsterdam he was turned over 'as a great favour' to his other uncle, the future Sir William Blackett. Perhaps because of his father's loyal service as an officer in the royalist army, William was made envoy to the Swedish court, where he stayed for many years and married the daughter of the duc de Boys. It seems probable, however, that he also engaged in trade during his time in Sweden, for we find a William Blackett taking a leading part in the export of iron from Sweden to England: 'In contrast to other merchants, Blackett did not buy iron from iron-works and he never engaged in the iron industry…he bought his iron in Stockholm from other iron exporters…He purchased huge volumes of bar iron and he paid well'.[78]

Although he returned to Tyneside, it was not William but his younger brother, John, who took over the Wylam estate. As a historian of the village of Wylam put it: '…in 1679 much of the land and property in the village was acquired by John Blackett of Horton Grange near Ponteland, so beginning an unbroken period of almost 300 years until 1971 during which the Blackett family were Lords of the Manor of Wylam'.[79]

Wylam was not a cohesive estate as there were a number of landowners within the manor, but John Blackett of Wylam Hall was not only lord of the manor but also the largest landowner. It is not clear how much land he inherited, for he seems to have bought more land from members of the Fenwick family at the time he moved to Wylam.

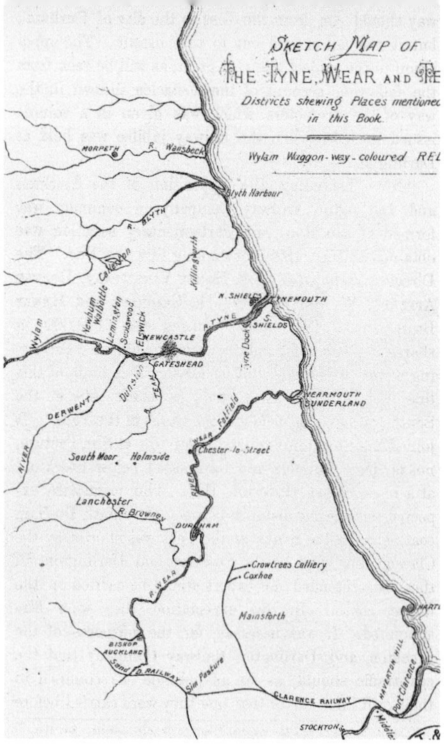

The Wylam Waggonway (marked in red) From M. Archer, *The Invention of Railway Locomotion on the Present Principle* (1882).

Before the dissolution of the monasteries, Wylam belonged to the Prior of Tynemouth. The Priory maintained a house at Wylam that was destroyed by the Scots in the early fourteenth century, but after it was rebuilt it was used by the monks as a 'sporting house' or hunting lodge. After the dissolution this house became Wylam Hall, and though it was transformed over the centuries, the medieval core of the house was retained.

Land at Wylam was not just valuable because of its agricultural potential. There was coal beneath it. The monks of Tynemouth had been early exploiters of coal seams near Tynemouth and they were mining at Wylam as early as 1292. Like the manor house, the coal mine passed through many hands, including those of the Fenwicks, until it eventually came to the Blacketts. John Blackett's son, another John, let Wylam Colliery in 1738, but the family continued to own it until the nineteenth century.

The Blacketts of Wylam have been described as 'generally unambitious sons of the soil, who lived on the paternal acres and married into other many acred families or went into the army'.[80] There is some truth in this description, for three successive John Blacketts married the daughters of prosperous local gentry families and all served as High Sheriff. The family, however, maintained its links with Newcastle and with mercantile life, engaged actively in trade, and owned the wine and spirit business Blackett and Dixon. Never wealthy on the scale of the Blacketts of Wallington or Matfen, they maintained their gentry status from generation to generation.

The family has also an important place in the history of coal-mining and in that of the railways, for which coal-mining was the midwife. During the mid-eighteenth

'Puffing Billy'.
Photograph courtesy of the Science Museum / Science and Society Picture Library.

century the Wylam Waggonway was constructed, one of the first in the north east, enabling coal to be transported between Wylam Colliery and the staithes at Lemington, whence keels could take it down river to sea-going vessels. In the early nineteenth century Wylam was to be at the centre of the development of the steam locomotive, with George Stephenson, William Hedley, Timothy Hackworth and Nicholas Wood all associated with the village. A crucial role was, however, played by the new lord of the manor, Christopher Blackett, who inherited the estate in 1800 following the successive deaths of two half-brothers who left no heirs.

In 1804 Christopher Blackett ordered a locomotive of the Trevithick type, which was built at a Gateshead foundry. Once it had been constructed, he refused to accept it, realizing that it was far too heavy for the wooden rails of his waggonway. Blackett and his viewer, William Hedley, persevered, however, relaying the railway with cast-iron-rails and experimenting with a locomotive that had a toothed driving wheel and was driven on a rack-rail. To keep their experiments from the public eye they utilized the drive to Wylam Hall, causing a great deal of damage to the drive in the process. These experiments proved a failure, so Hedley found a means of measuring the tractive power of smooth wheels upon smooth rails and constructed his first successful locomotive, the 'Wylam Dilly', followed by the 'Puffing Billy'. By 1815 locomotives were hauling wagons along the five-mile track to Lemington Staithes.

Hedley's role in the invention of steam locomotives has been unfairly overshadowed by the achievements of Trevithick and Stephenson. As a doughty Victorian supporter of Hedley wrote:

...five miles of rough wagon-way, from Wylam to Lemington, bore the first of those wonderful iron-horses that now inhabit the world, the willing servants of civilization and commerce everywhere. There are many famous dates and famous places, but, if we consider the mighty changes effected by the introduction of locomotives, all resulting from William Hedley's ingenuity and Mr Blackett's undaunted support, we may reasonably ask what date and what place are more worthy of fame than May 1813, and the old waggonway from Wylam to the Tyne.[81]

St Oswin's Church at Wylam was built in memory of William Hedley, and a tablet commemorates his and Christopher Blackett's achievement:

To the inventive genius of William Hedley at Wylam in 1812, and assisted by the perseverance of the late Christopher Blackett, Esqr., (at whose expense the experiments were made) the world is indebted for the first successful Locomotive Steam Engine.

Due in part to these innovations, Wylam Colliery, which with other Blackett pits on the south side of the river made up one complex, seems to have thrived. Eneas McKenzie, in his history of Northumberland, published in 1825, described the workings:

The coal is worked on the south side of the Tyne, conveyed by rail under the river and drawn up here and from hence sent by locomotive engines by a railway to Lemington, a distance of above five miles...sometimes a dozen or more wagons are drawn by one engine.[82]

While Christopher Blackett was contributing to Britain's industrial history, his son, another Christopher, was serving with Wellington's army and fighting his way through Portugal, Spain and France with the 18th Hussars. He married Elizabeth Burgoyne in 1818 and, after his father's death, lived at Wylam.

Although descended from the same seventeenth-century family and owning near adjacent estates, the Blacketts of Wylam and their relatives at Matfen do not seem to have been particularly involved with one another during the latter part of the eighteenth century or, indeed, later in the nineteenth century. Alethea Blackett, though otherwise exhaustive in her pursuit of family connections, hardly mentions them. In the early nineteenth century, however, the young Christopher Blackett does seem to have been on close terms with the Matfen Blacketts. 'Kit' corresponded regularly with Sir William Blackett, 5th Bt., and his wife, Mary-Anne, and was also a good friend of their son Sir Edward Blackett, 6th Bt.

Christopher was the first member of his line to have political ambitions and was elected in 1830 as MP for Beer Alston in Devon, along with Lord Lovaine, the son of the Duke of Northumberland. Beer Alston was a pocket borough of the Percys and was to be abolished by the Great Reform Act. Christopher Blackett was its MP for only a few months and was not a candidate in the 1831 election. Perhaps he was already moving towards a Whig or even a radical position, for in 1836, after the death of one of the sitting members, Sir Matthew White Ridley, he contested Newcastle with the support of Whigs and radicals. Standing for a major urban constituency like Newcastle must have been a very different experience from being effortlessly conveyed to parliament by Beer Alston's hundred voters, but Blackett fought hard, backed by the liberal luminaries of the town and losing by forty-eight votes in a poll of 3104. The following year he was elected unopposed for South Northumberland, but had to retire because of ill health in 1841, six years before his death.

Christopher's younger brother, John Alexander, became a clergyman and was Vicar of Heddon-on-the-Wall. His wife's mother was the eldest sister of William Ord MP of Whitfield Hall (whose widow became Sir Edward Blackett's second wife), and when Ord died without having children, his niece succeeded to his estate and John Alexander changed his name from Blackett to Blackett-Ord.

Christopher Blackett's son, John Fenwick Burgoyne Blackett, Fellow of Merton College, Oxford, a barrister and a contributor to leading Liberal journals, was in the 1850s the rising star of north-east Liberalism and seemed destined for a great political career. He was elected MP for Newcastle in 1852 with a huge majority, amid encomia to his exemplary qualities. An advanced Liberal, he made a great impression in the House of Commons, championing political reform in India, Italian unity, and educational reform of Oxford and Cambridge. His burgeoning political career was, however, cut short by poor health; he retired from parliament in 1856 after only one term and died shortly afterwards.

The Blacketts were popular in Wylam and its environs. Ever since the early eighteenth century, when John Blackett gave £6 per annum to be distributed yearly on All Saints' Day to the poor by the minister and churchwardens of Ovingham, they had proved to be generous landlords. John Fenwick Burgoyne Blackett was a paternalistic squire, building a British School and a Reading Institute for the village. They possessed two large houses, Wylam Hall (it had earlier been known as Wylam House) and Oakwood House.

Top right: Wylam Hall, photographed in the 1960s. *Photograph courtesy of Philip Brooks.*

Bottom right: Oakwood. *Photograph courtesy of Philip Brooks.*

OAKWOOD HALL. WYLAM

136 Christopher Blackett (1751–1829).
Photograph courtesy of the Science Museum / Science and Society Picture Library.

From the 1820s Wylam Hall was leased for much of the time. For a while it was rented by Edward James, who ran the Ouseburn Lead Company. George Clayton Atkinson, industrialist and naturalist, lived there for twenty years between 1854 and 1874, being followed as tenant by Captain Richard Clayton, who, after an adventurous military career, became a leading banker in Newcastle. Clayton leased the house for twenty-one years in 1891 for £240 a year and added an extension to the west of the house.

Oakwood House seems to have been built about the mid-eighteenth century, and is shown on the earliest detailed map of Wylam, of 1766, as belonging to a Robert Swallow. By 1793 Thomas Blackett, then lord of the manor, was living there, and the Blacketts seem to have preferred it to Wylam Hall, residing there during the first half of the nineteenth century. It was leased to Norman C. Cookson for £25 a year in 1877, and his widow lived there until 1923.[83]

After J.F.B. Blackett's death the lords of the manor were by no means consistently resident in Wylam. Captain Edward Algernon Blackett RN, who succeeded his brother, was a Deputy Lord Lieutenant and a JP for Northumberland but, after he married the daughter of an Irish clergyman, he spent much of his time in Ireland. He inherited an estate in County Tipperary, and the heads of the family were thereafter described as 'of Wylam, Oakwood and Barnagrotty'.

Edward Algernon's son, Colonel Edward Umfraville Blackett, pursued a military career in the Royal Artillery and was for many years posted to India. When he was on leave, he visited Wylam to consult with his agent and see to his interests there, but otherwise divided his time between London and Ireland, and sojourns in France and Italy. He had no children by his first marriage, but a son and two daughters by his second, to a cousin, the second daughter of Sir Vincent Rowland Corbet, a marriage that brought him the estate of Exton in Staffordshire. After his military career Colonel Blackett spent more time at Wylam and added a new wing to Wylam Hall in 1912–13.

Edward Umfraville's son, Christopher John Walter Blackett, was the last male in the direct line and was described by *Burke's Landed Gentry* as 'of Wylam, Northumberland, Barnagrotty, Tipperary, and Exton, North Staffs'. Born in 1900 he succeeded his father at the age of twenty; he was a popular and public-spirited squire, who served as a member of the Rural District Council and did much for charitable causes in Wylam. He died without an heir in 1971. The Wylam estate was largely sold off, and three hundred years of a paternalistic Blackett squirearchy came to an end.

4. THE HOUSES TODAY

Willimoteswick.

The world that Alethea, Lady Blackett, knew may, like the history she sought to recapture, have passed. Yet far more of the scenery and houses she painted and photographed remains than we might expect. The north east of England has its share of 'lost houses', while industry and urban development have encroached on countryside, destroying fine landscapes and parklands; but much of rural Northumberland and North Yorkshire remains relatively unspoiled. Probably more great houses there are intact, with the landscapes around them still recognizable from what they were in their heyday, than in other parts of modern England.

Anderson Place is, of course, long gone. An anomaly for decades before its demise, with its thirteen acres in the midst of densely populated Newcastle, it was pulled down to make way for Dobson's and Grainger's magnificent development of the town in the 1830s. We can trace only the outlines of the house and the grounds where the Blacketts strolled and so lavishly entertained, but here at least there was gain for loss.[84]

A more recent casualty was Bonny Rigg Hall. This fine Dobson house in its magnificent, wild setting remained in the Blackett family until the late 1960s. It was burned down in 1985. Until the 1930s Bonny Rigg and its shooting were maintained in the old manner, with a head keeper and several other gamekeepers permanently based there. The family moved there for the grouse shooting and to holiday every August. Sir Hugh Blackett remembers his father, Sir Francis, telling him how he and his brothers would set off on their ponies to ride there along the military road. In 1932, however, Sir Hugh Douglas Blackett was ill and was not able to come to Bonny Rigg for the shooting, which seems thereafter to have been let out and the

Blacketts not to have come so regularly.[85] Nevertheless, the family seem to have returned to their previous routine in the post-war period. Valerie Gibson, who has lived close to Bonny Rigg since the 1950s, recalls that the gardeners from Matfen would arrive a week or two beforehand to put the extensive gardens in order before the arrival of the family and its guests. The Hall and the surrounding farms were, however, sold off to pay death duties after Sir Charles Douglas Blackett's death in 1968. The creation of the Northumberland National Park afforded protection for Bonny Rigg and the whole of the Forest of Lowes, as the area was once called (the name is said to refer to the land of lakes or loughs), from unsuitable development. There also seemed to be a promise of sustainable and sympathetic development, with Bonny Rigg becoming the headquarters of a sailing club set up on Greenlee Lough. The Blacketts had sold the hall with a lease they had agreed with the club but, partly owing to the development of the Derwent Reservoir as a sailing centre that offered much easier access, the club at Greenlee Lough closed. Then came the fire. The walls of the Hall were left standing and there was a possibility that it could have been repaired but, rather precipitately, the owner had the building levelled on the grounds that it was in a dangerous condition. Only the stable

Left: The site of Bonny Rigg Hall today.

Right: Prior's House, Hexham. The building now houses a magistrates court, Northumberland County Council Social Services and a doctor's surgery.

Overleaf: Halton Tower.

block survived the fire and now forms two cottages. The lough remains, however, as it was when Alethea Blackett painted it, mercurial in its rapid changes from placid lake on the rare still day to its wild and windswept normal self.

Prior's House or Abbey House in Hexham was a fine house in Sir Walter Blackett's day, and the additions by Sir Reginald Carnaby, along with Sir Walter's own improvements, made it a fitting residence for the lord of the manor. As we have seen Sir Walter laid out the grounds, in which he allowed the townsfolk to stroll with trees and walkways. The fire in 1775, two years before Sir Walter's death, destroyed much of the older part of the building, including the battlements and turrets. Although the structure was lavishly rebuilt, two further fires in 1817 and 1818 necessitated a further rebuilding on a more modest scale, leaving Prior's House much as it is today. The description of it by A.B. Wright in his *History of Hexham* (1823) as 'a mean building, every way unworthy of its name and situation, and its appearance does little credit either to the taste or liberality of the proprietor' seems harsh. It would have taken a very great architect to build a mansion in the shadow of the abbey that could receive the applause of antiquarians. Soon afterwards the Beaumonts ceased to use the house as a residence. It provided lodging for judges and then became a Court House for the Petty Sessions and the County Courts, its fine ballroom proving adequate as a Court Room. In the twentieth century Wentworth Canning Beaumont, 2nd Baron and 1st Viscount Allendale, Hexham's great benefactor, presented the seal – a stretch of land beside the Abbey – to the town and disposed of the abbey building to the County Council, that the grounds 'might remain a park for ever'.

Left: The colonnade presented to Hexham by Sir Walter Blackett.

Right: Aydon Castle. *Photograph courtesy of English Heritage Photographic Library.*

As modest trees often withstand the storm better than great oaks, so small manors can survive the gales of centuries better than grand mansions. Willimoteswick and Halton Tower not only survive, but fulfil at least part of their original functions: if their defensive capabilities are no longer required, they are both still private residences with farmland stretching around them. They are also, in terms of architectural history, two of the most important houses in Northumberland.

Willimoteswick lies where the northern slopes of the Pennines reach down to the valley of the south Tyne and where moorland meets gentler pastures, a fine position for the view in modern terms, just as it was once a fine position from which to observe the movements of potential enemies. Many features of this small fortified manor would still be recognizable to the Ridleys, who possessed it until the Civil War, for of the hall and the cross-wings with towers the east wing and its tower survive, as does the fortified gatehouse to the north east. Early twentieth-century alterations, albeit in sixteenth-century style, have changed much of the rest of the building, though the re-use of original materials and doorways makes all seem well aged. Augustus Hare described it in his *Murray's Handbook of Northumberland*: 'It forms the entrance of a farmyard, [and] is picturesquely covered with yellow lichens'. The house may have changed a little over time, but for all its present tranquillity it still stands as a reminder of the need for defence that characterized Northumberland's architecture for so many centuries.

Halton Tower (or Castle) has changed little, at least in essentials, since John Douglas attached a late seventeenth-century house to the fourteenth-century tower. With the tall beech hedges protecting its gardens, and its church close by, Halton is

Wallington today: the garden front, taken from the south. *National Trust Photographic Library/(Marianne Majerus).*

secluded and peaceful, approached by winding lanes or the private drive that slopes down from the military road, and the Roman fort of Haltonchesters, whence came much of the masonry that was used to build the house.

The two houses belonging to the Blacketts of Wylam, Wylam Hall and Oakwood House, are both extant. Wylam Hall is now divided into a number of flats and is much smaller, as the south wing, the oldest part of the house, was destroyed by fire in 1964, but Oakwood remains a single private residence.

Four of the houses that we have discussed are in their different ways open to the public: Aydon Castle, Wallington Hall, Newby Hall and Matfen Hall.

A contemporary of Alethea Blackett, William Weaver Tomlinson, wrote of Aydon Castle (or Aydon Hall as it was originally known) that it:

> *...occupies a position of great strength and beauty above the well-wooded slope of a charming little dene, through which the Cor wanders musically on its way to the Tyne. It is at present a better-class farmhouse, though still retaining many of its ancient features.*'[86]

So Aydon remained until comparatively recently, when the Ministry of Works and then English Heritage decided to remove as much as possible of later alterations to the Hall, in order to reveal what remains of the thirteenth-century fortified manor house and the fourteenth-century additions. If, as the latest Pevsner says, this gives 'a slightly gutted feel to the interiors',[87] it does enable us to appreciate what is, for Northumberland, an unusual house. Undefended manor houses were

Newby Hall.
Reproduced by kind permission of Mr. Richard Compton.

common enough further south in England in the thirteenth century, but were rare indeed so close to the border. They were to remain so for several centuries after Aydon was first built, for the comparative calm of twelfth-century Northumberland was to be rudely broken at the end of the thirteenth century by the devastation inflicted by the Scots under William Wallace. Defence in much of the county would have to take precedence over gracious living until the Union of the Crowns.

The fortification of Aydon in the early fourteenth century bears witness to this. By the time of the manor's acquisition by John Douglas, which was followed by its transmission by marriage to the Blacketts, the need for defence had passed and, because the Blacketts had no real need for Aydon as a manor house, it became a grand, if not very comfortable or practical, farmhouse, remaining as such until the Blackett family handed it over to the Ministry of Works in 1966. English Heritage now looks after the deconstructed medieval building. It is a house that can be appreciated by visitors in several ways: for its magnificent situation, for its historic and architectural importance, for its mellow walls and for a peacefulness that belies its bloody past.

Wallington is the most popular of National Trust houses in the north east. It remained the private home of the Trevelyans until the death of Sir Charles Trevelyan in 1958. A Liberal and then a Labour MP, Minister for Education in the first two Labour governments, Sir Charles left Wallington to the National Trust. James Lees-Milne, who handled the Trust's side of the negotiations and who disliked 'the rather etiolated left-wing essence prevalent throughout the donors' regime', [88] has provided a wonderfully satirical account of his visits during the protracted transaction that preceded the handover.

That Wallington is more associated in the minds of visitors with the Trevelyans than with their predecessors, the Blacketts, is understandable. The Trevelyan family inhabited the house until the National Trust took over. Their furniture and possessions are still there and something of the aura of the Trevelyans still surrounds the house. The essential design of Wallington and the layout of the grounds, and indeed, the surrounding landscape, are, nevertheless, the work of Sir William Blackett, 1st Bt. of Wallington, and of Sir Walter Calverley Blackett.

Newby Hall, the house built for Sir Edward Blackett, is the property of the Compton family, the heirs of the Weddells, who bought it from the Blacketts in the mid-eighteenth century. If the exterior of the main house remains largely as it was when it was built in the late seventeenth century, the glorious interior is due to William Weddell. A man of great taste, whose education was polished by the Grand Tour, Weddell was a prominent member of the Dilettanti Society and employed the leading neo-classical architects of the day to extend and modify the house, but the great achievement was the transformation of the interior by Robert Adam. Newby Hall is a monument to the taste and sensibility of the eighteenth-century aristocracy: the entrance hall is a dream of ancient Rome; the gallery room is consciously based on the Tribune of the Uffizi Gallery in Florence and contains the statuary William acquired on the Grand Tour; the tapestry room is adorned with the work of the Gobelins factory; and the dining room, since 1807 the library, decorated by Adam, provides a wonderful context for Angelica Kauffman's oval painting of *Bacchus and Ariadne* on the ceiling. With all its artistic magnificence, Newby manages to combine, as do so many great English country houses, domesticity with grandeur: the feeling that this was a house in which the owners lived comfortably, surrounded but not overawed by the projection of their wealth and taste.

Newby is an example of that compromise that makes visiting great English houses so popular, a lived-in family home that is open to the public. The Compton family have added to the attractions of the house, parkland and extensive gardens a Woodland Discovery Walk, Adventure Gardens and a miniature railway that runs alongside the river.

The problem of the great country houses of England, along with warnings of their imminent demise, has been discussed ever since the 1920s. With Wallington and Newby, we see two possible solutions, the public trusteeship and the marketing of the house's attractions by the owners. Many other houses were sold over the years and became the headquarters of businesses or residential homes for the elderly, the sick or the infirm. This was not usually the happiest of fates for houses, once the hub of surrounding communities. In many ways the houses became more private than they had ever been and interiors were destroyed to suit the needs of the new owners.

Matfen Hall, with the church and village behind.

Matfen Hall was luckier than most in that, when the Blackett family found the house impractical and too expensive to maintain as their principal home in the 1960s, it was let at a peppercorn rent to Cheshire Homes in return for the sensitive maintenance of house and grounds. As a Cheshire Home, Matfen provided a comfortable and spacious environment for its residents, and offered what the house had always given, employment to the locality. By the 1990s, however, Cheshire Homes, like similar foundations, was altering its policies, and concluded that urban locations were more suitable for its purposes. Sir Hugh Blackett, who inherited the baronetcy in 1995, decided upon a different future for the house and grounds.

Were Sir Edward Blackett or his fourth wife, Alethea, to be able to make a posthumous visit to Matfen Hall, they would find much that was instantly recognizable. The house and its principal rooms resemble closely the detailed descriptions given by Lady Alethea, while the terraces, gardens, walkways and vistas are much as they were a century and a half ago. It is likely that Sir Edward would wonder what all those little flags dotted around the park were, and he might be surprised at the number of guests, even though he used to entertain so many himself. He would undoubtedly be impressed by the service and the quality of the food, and would conclude that his descendants had found a good butler. In its new incarnation as a golf course, hotel, conference centre, venue for weddings, and health and fitness centre, Matfen Hall puts the nineteenth-century house and older parkland to excellent use. The carefully designed parks of English country houses, with their fine trees and copses and their lakes and streams, make challenging and scenic golf courses, though the golfer who finds his ball close to the green but

The 'ghost of Matfen' in the Gothic Hall, 1995.

at the base of a ha-ha might not always admire the ingenuity of a bygone landscape gardener. The country house hotel emerges effortlessly from the country house, with its gracious drawing rooms, imposing library and wide terrace overlooking the River Pont. As for the Gothic Hall, what better setting for a marriage!

Every serious country house should have a ghost, and a standard ghost is a 'grey lady'. Matfen is no exception, though the ghost is not well documented, and no-one seems to have seen her for many years: probably a myth or a tale made up to frighten junior servants has been the general assumption. Yet recently, a photographer was commissioned to take some promotional pictures, including a photograph of the monumental fireplace in the Gothic Hall. He saw nothing untoward through the lens, but when the film was developed, there was the figure of a lady, her face framed by the hood of her cloak. Is this a trick of the light or a retiring and well-behaved ghost, who did little to disturb generations of Blacketts and seems content merely to observe the busy new Matfen Hall?

Newcastle's prosperity was built upon trade, and merchants provided its dynamism. William Blackett's adventurous investment in the risky flax trade was a crucial step in a brilliant business career. Many built up solid fortunes, but Blackett scaled the dizziest heights and bestrode the town, achieving an almost princely position. His successors retained their links with the town, but bought land and established themselves in magnificent country houses. Guests at Matfen Hall today, visitors to Wallington and Newby Hall, and Hexham residents, who pass the *piazza* in the market place, or stroll in Beaumont Park, have reason to be glad that William Blackett's ship came home.

NOTES

1. She was the great-great-granddaughter of Christopher Blackett, son of John Blackett of Newby Hall, as well as great-granddaughter of Christopher's nephew Sir Edward Blackett (1719–1804).
2. The work of Mark Blackett-Ord, compiler of the entries on Sir William and his son Sir Edward Blackett in Oxford University Press's *New Dictionary of National Biography*, has provided me with much information on the early history of the Blackett family.
3. John Straker, Pedigree of the Family of Blackett, Newcastle Typographical Society (1829), p. 27.
4. M.A. Richardson, *Reprints of Rare Tracts* (1847).
5. R. Welford, *Men of Mark 'Twixt Tyne and Tweed* (1865).
6. The Reverend John Brand, *The History and Antiquities of the Town and County of Newcastle upon Tyne*, 2 vols. (Newcastle, 1789).
7. He was married to the daughter, by her first marriage, of the second wife of Sir William Blackett (1621–1680).
8. Newcastle's MPs were: 1685 Nathaniel Johnson and Sir William Blackett; 1689 Sir Ralph Carr and Sir William Blackett; 1695 William Carr and Sir William Blackett; 1698 William Carr and Sir William Blackett; 1705 William Carr and Sir William Blackett. On Blackett's death he was succeeded by Sir Henry Liddell.
9. 'Obsequies of certain of the family of Blackett of Newcastle' in M.A. Richardson, *Reprints of Rare Tracts* (1847).
10. Brand, *op. cit.*, vol. I, p. 341.
11. Welford, *op. cit.*, vol. I 1895, p. 303.
12. Sir Charles Trevelyan, *Wallington* (London, 1930), p. 10.
13. '...10s per diem for each man & horse & Charges, for as many days as they shall be in their Journey Outward and comeing Back allowing and agreed for: 20 upon the whole at 6*l* per day, 120*l*.' A proposal and agreement made for [part of the expenses of] the Funerall of the Hon Sir William Blackett Bt, Richardson's *Reprints* vol. V, p. 24.
14. Henry Liddell to Wiliam Cotesworth, 10 October. 1715, *Liddell-Cotesworth Letters, Surtees Society* (1987 ed. Joyce Ellis), vol. CXCVII, p. 183.
15. John Hodgson, *History of Northumberland*, vol. II (Newcastle, 1820–40), p. 269.
16. L. Gooch, *The Desperate Faction. The Jacobites of North-East England 1685–1745* (casdec, Birtley, County Durham, 2001), p. 53.
17. Liddell to Cotesworth, 4 January 1716, *Liddell-Cotesworth Letters* p. 212.
18. Poem by William Robson of Cambo.
19. Poem by Tom Whittle.
20. Bond for Life. NRO ZBL 35/3.
21. Declaration of 1 September 1711 by Thomas Davidson that £7600 is the total sum owed to them from Sir William Blackett, deceased. Agreement of 19 March 1724 by which Thomas Guy of Lombard Street London pays to the Davidsons their £7600 out of a new mortgage of £65,000 on security of a great part of his estates in Northumberland and Durham to Thomas Guy, subject to a condition contained in a mortgage of 7 March 1724 to Lancelot Allgood. Shafto Papers, University of Durham, Nos. 281 and 297.
22. Hodgson, *op. cit.*, p. 272.
23. Blackett to Allgood, 9 June 1747.
24. Welford, *op. cit.*, p. 216.
25. Trevelyan, *op. cit.*, p. 19.
26. W. Hutchinson, *A View of the County of Northumberland*, 2 vols. (1778), p. 99.
27. Hodgson, *op. cit.*, p. 261.
28. Taken from the extracts that Lady Blackett copied out from *The Life of Reverend Alexander Carlyle.*
29. Edward Grierson, *Northumbria* (Collins, 1976), p. 142.
30. Letter from one P. Poynings quoted in Raleigh Trevelyan, *Wallington* (National Trust, 1994), p. 16
31. *ibid.*, p.15.
32. Sir Walter's estate was encumbered by debts, annuities for life and allowances. These amounted in all to £86,423 principal and £3,609 interest. 'A schedule for Sir Walter Blackett's debts', NRO 5327.
33. Thomas Faulkner and Andrew Greg, *John Dobson. Architect of the North East* (Tyne Bridge Publishing, 2001), pp. 43–4.
34. *Newcastle Chronicle*, (5 July 1794).
35. Copied by Alethea, Lady Blackett, from *The Memoirs of Anna Maria Pickering*, edited by her son, Spencer Pickering (1903.
36. Letter from Mary Russell Mitford quoted in Hinds, *History of Northumberland*, vol. III, 1896, p. 261.
37. The real cause of the quarrel was not politics but Beaumont's allegations that Lady Swinburne had been unfaithful to her husband with Earl Grey (Howick's father), General Grey, and her butler.
38. F.W. Dendy, *Extracts from the Records of the Hostmen's Company of Newcastle upon Tyne* vol. I, 1901 (1987, ed. Joyce Ellis), pp. 291–2.
39. Alethea Blackett refers to his purchase of 'Newby Grange'.
40. A detailed account of Aram's work at Newby Hall is contained in Frank Finkelstein, 'Aram's Practical Treatise of Flowers', Leeds Literary and Philosophical Society.
41. Celia Fiennes, *The Journeys of Celia Fiennes (*Macdonald, 1983), pp. 105–6.
42. Draft of entry for *New DNB* by Mark Blackett-Ord.
43. Francis Askham, *The Gay Delavals* (Jonathan Cape, 1955), p. 21.
44. Christopher Blackett's son, a clergyman, left all his property to his godson, Edward Scott, and the property eventually came to General Scott, the father of the family historian, Alethea Blackett. Christopher's daughter, Julia, married a Scott, and their son, William, who became a general, married Anne, the daughter of Sir Edward Blackett, 4th Bt. Alethea Blackett's father, another General Scott, was their son. Most authorities suggest that it was Henry, the sixth son of Sir Edward, who married Jane Saville, and that Christopher, the fifth son, died young. I follow Alethea Blackett, who should have known her own family history, in stating the opposite.
45. He was later to be Chancellor of the Exchequer and had to resign in disgrace after the 'South Sea Bubble' burst.
46. The family had expected that, as Sir William Blackett had no legitimate children, the

Wallington and Hexham estates would come to them. However, as we have seen, they went to Sir Walter Calverley.

47. At the time of the Act of Parliament that gave consent to the marriage, Anne Douglas's estate was estimated to be worth £2211 p.a.
48. The whole estate in 1759 was reckoned to be worth upwards of £5000 a year. Sir Edward had added Matfen, Halton, Aydon, Carr-houses, and Whittington to the family estates, which included Horneby in Yorkshire, the manor of Sockburn in Durham, and the manors and lordships of Willimoteswick, Chesterwood, Ridley and Ridley Hall, Thorngrafton, Henshaw, Huntlands, Kingswood and Melkridge and certain lands in these manors, and in Dinsdale Bishopton, the Forest of Lowes, Fallowfield, Woodhall and Winlaton.
49. Hutchinson, *op. cit.*, p. 142.
50. Peter Ryder, 'Halton Castle', *Archaeology in Northumberland 2000–2001* (Northumberland County Council), p. 29.
51. Alethea Blackett, unpublished manuscript.
52. The Fenwicks seem to have owned almost every house in Northumberland at one time or another and to have lost nearly all of them.
53. John Wallis (Northumberland, 1769).
54. Hutchinson, *op. cit.*, pp. 135–6.
55. Reverend Alexander Carlyle, *Autobiography Containing Memorials of the Men and Events of his Time* (Edinburgh, 1860), p. 412.
56. *ibid.*, p. 417. This was one of the few things on which Carlyle and Mrs Montague, the Queen of the Blue Stockings, whose London salon was much frequented by intellectuals of the period, agreed. She owned Denton Hall and its adjacent coal mines, just outside Newcastle, and complained that conversation in Newcastle was limited 'as it always turns upon money'. Carlyle, however, found her pretentious.
57. This was rather hard on a man who had been a most efficient agent. He had driven hard bargains on his employers' behalf and there was a long drawn out court case, the Bishop of Durham *v* Sir Thomas Blackett, in which J.E. Blackett was accused of misrepresenting the real value of a lead mine in Weardale and thus defrauding the bishop of his rightful profits.
58. Oliver Warner, *Life and Letters of Vice-Admiral Lord Collingwood* (Oxford University Press, 1968), p. 121.
59. Sir Edward Blackett to Patience Scott *c.*1801. Alethea Blackett's MS.
60. *ibid.*, William Scott to Sir Edward Blackett, 28 April 1799.
61. John Ridley to Lady Blackett, 12 January 1819, Alethea Blackett's MS. The public road ran past the stables and was detoured along its present path.
62. Diaries of Sir Edward Blackett, 6th Bt, Northumberland Record Office (ZBL 266).
63. Faulkner and Greg, *op. cit.*, pp. 76 and 79.
64. Alethea Blackett's MS.
65. Alethea Blackett's MS.
66. Una Pope-Henessy, *Durham Company* (Chatto and Windus, 1941), p.109.
67. Alethea Blackett's MS.
68. Robert Newton, *The Northumberland Landscape* (Hodder and Stoughton, 1972), p. 202.
69. N. Pevsner and I.A. Richmond, *The Buildings of England, Northumberland* (1957), p. 210; 2nd edition, revised by John Grundy *et al* (Penguin, 1992), p. 387.
70. W.W.Tomlinson, *Comprehensive Guide to Northumberland* (1888, revised David and Charles, 1968), p.147.
71. *Mistress of Charlecote. The Memoirs of Mary Elizabeth Lucy*, introduced by Alice Fairfax Lucy (Gollancz, 1983), pp. 161–2. Baroness Burdett-Coutts had inherited the Coutts banking fortune.
72. To make things even more complicated, Alethea's aunt, Anne Scott, had married the comte de Roullee, who, after her death, married Sir Edward's sister, Patience Maria.
73. Catherine Cookson's own experience of illegitimacy in an urban context probably led her to exaggerate its horrors in the countryside, where there was a much more matter of fact attitude to it. Corbridge, close to Matfen, had, for instance, a notoriously high illegitimacy rate, which the majority of villagers seem just to have accepted.
74. Sir William Blackett of Wallington had maintained a shooting lodge at Blackhall Hill near Simonside, built *c.*1700, and it is often asserted that Wallington itself was originally purchased as a shooting lodge.
75. The desire of his gamekeepers to satisfy Sir Edward's eagerness to have plenty of game to shoot made them, perhaps, over-enthusiastic about destroying predators. There was a great row when his keepers destroyed a colony of black-headed gulls at Grindon Lough, an action that was attacked by the Tyneside Naturalists' Field Club and its president, fellow Northumberland landowner Ralph Carr.
76. W.H. Scott to his wife, 27 August (year unknown but *c.* 1860).
77. W.H. Scott to his wife, 21 and 27 August 1862.
78. Leos Muller, 'Britain and Sweden: the Changing Pattern of Commodity Exchange, 1650–1680', in *Britain and the Baltic*, eds Patrick Salmon and Tony Barrow (Sunderland University Press, 2003), p. 69.
79. Philip R.B. Brooks, *Wylam Past. A Pictorial History of a Northumberland Village* (Northumberland Library, 1998).
80. Welford, *op. cit.*, vol. I, p. 319.
81. M. Archer, *The Invention of Railway Locomotion on the Present Principle* (1882, p. 21).
82. E. McKenzie, *Northumberland* (Newcastle, 1825), p. 372.
83. Brooks, *op. cit.*
84. Thorpe Lea, far away from the Northumberland houses of the Blacketts, had to be pulled down to make way for the M25.
85. Based on a manuscript, 'A description of Bonny Rigg', by Ninian Carr.
86. W.W. Tomlinson, *op. cit.*, p. 141.
87. Pevsner, *op. cit.*, p. 149.
88. James Lees-Milne, *People and Places. Country House Donors and the National Trust* (John Murray, 1992), p. 164.

INDEX

GUNS

6.
J. C. Straker, W. Allgood
A. Blackett R. Blackett.
2.61. Mr Perkat & Self.

5.
J. C. Straker W. Allgood.
A. H. Straker B. Allgood & Self.

4.
H. L. Medlicott

21. H. & B. RB & Self.

3.
H. L. Medlicott

6. RB & Self.

7.
A. H. Middleton Mr C. E. Blackett
L. W. " Mr Liddell
M. Fenwick L. Fenwick & Self.
44.

4.

55. C. G. Barnett. HLB. RB Self.

8.
Sir A. Middleton L. Dent.
H. J. " Ridley
Jackson Blackett & Self.
71. Jackson

1.

12. Self.

6.
J. Blackett-Ord. A. Ridley
L. Middleton C. A. Hope Wallace
40. H. L. ... & Self.

lost in the morning then later.

lost a very bad light
saw very few birds.

afternoon only.
snipe very wild.

gale of wind.

lost & foggy.